ENCOURAGEMENT IN

ENCOURAGEMENT IN DARK DAYS

THE VISIONS OF ZECHARIAH

William Macleod

Foreword by the Rev. Maurice J. Roberts

Scottish Reformed Heritage Publications
2023

Scripture quotations
are taken from the King James Version (KJV).

Cover Picture Credit: Part of the old city
of Jerusalem (Rev. John W. Keddie)

ISBN: 978-1-4477-7526-3

Publisher:
Scottish Reformed Heritage Publications
19 Newton Park
Kirkhill
Inverness-shire
IV5 7QB

Printed by Lulu (www.lulu.com)

CONTENTS

FOREWORD

CHRISTIANS today need spiritual encouragement. It is this which is offered in this excellent book. It is today a dark day and believers need heaven-sent biblical light to comfort them. It is by opening to us wonderful passages in the prophecy of Zechariah that the Rev. William Macleod gives us this comfort. The Old Testament is God's inspired word to saints of both Old Testament and New.

God's people, nowadays, are saddened, as were His people in Old Testament times. Today churches are poorly attended, the Bible is not respected as God's Word and the Lord Jesus Christ is not believed by many to be our glorious Saviour.

William Macleod expounds most helpfully eight heavenly visions found in the first six chapters of the book of the prophet Zechariah. The exposition of these visions shows us how far society has fallen away from God in our Western world. But, more still, we are shown how Jesus Christ always is and will be the solution to mankind's sin and pride.

This book is based on ten lectures on these visions originally given by William Macleod to the John Knox Institute and available on its website (https://www.johnknoxinstitute.org).

I heartily recommend that this excellent book be read and made the subject of meditation. The unfolding of precious truths in Zechariah exposes the serious nature of modern atheism, materialism and "science falsely so called." The answer to the evils of Zechariah's day, as it is here shown, is the same as for our own day, in which unbelieving secularism is everywhere to be seen. The answer, then and now, is in these two vital subjects:

(1) The Bible as God's inspired Word;

(2) Jesus Christ, the Saviour of our souls.

This is the emphasis which this excellent book sets before us all, from start to finish!

Maurice J. Roberts

ENCOURAGEMENT IN DARK DAYS

CHAPTER 1

INTRODUCTION: GOD SPEAKS

(Zechariah 1:1-6)

As I have recently retired after having been a minister for many years, someone asked me which was my favourite book of the Bible. I have of course many favourites, as the Bible is a treasure trove. But he meant: from which book of the Bible did I particularly enjoy preaching. I replied that it was the prophecy of Zechariah. Why would that be the case? Zechariah is not a well-known Bible book. It has some passages which are difficult to interpret. There are strange visions in it. However, there are many things in this book which are plain and easily understood. Also, this prophecy of Zechariah is full of Christ. There is nothing more important for the Christian than Christ. Getting to know Him, trust Him and love Him is the way to be saved and once we have been saved, becomes the passion of our lives. In all their preaching, pastors are specially to preach Christ (Acts 2; Acts 17:3; 1 Corinthians 1:23; Ephesians 3:8, etc.). The Bible, both in the Old Testament as well as the New, is really all about Him. The Old Testament prepares for the coming of Christ. From the third chapter in Genesis onwards there are prophecies of the coming Messiah. The priesthood, the tabernacle and the sacrifices were types and symbols of the coming Saviour. The Gospels tell of His actual coming, death and resurrection. The Book of Acts describes the growth and spread of His church. The Epistles explain who Christ is and what our response should be to His atoning death. Then the Book of Revelation describes the future and Christ's second coming.

The prophecy of Zechariah is to be found at the end of the Old Testament dispensation. It is the second last book of the Old Testament and is anticipating the coming of the Messiah. It was a dark and difficult time for God's people. They were in a low state spiritually. The visions and words of Zechariah were given to encourage God's people to persevere through these dark times. God, through Zechariah, presents an optimistic view of the future, valuable not just to the Jews 2,500 years ago, but also to us today. The book calls on the Jews to return to God and God will return to them. It proclaims that God is in control. He is ruling the nations and the future for His church is bright and encouraging. Eight wonderful visions are given in the first six chapters. I would like in this book to consider these visions with you. I believe they will be a great encouragement and blessing to you, as they are also to myself. This chapter will be an introduction to these visions.

The very name of the prophet who wrote this book is significant. The name "Zechariah" means "Jehovah remembers." That is wonderful. We are tempted to think that God is far away. We feel at times that He has forgotten us. In our unbelief we fail to see that He is actively delivering His church. The cause of God in some places is very weak. Maybe we feel that God is asleep. No! Think of the name of the prophet. Jehovah, the covenant-keeping God, remembers. How could He ever forget! He is the God that cannot lie. He has entered into a covenant with His people and is bound to save them and bless them. "Can a woman forget her sucking child, that she should not have compassion on the son of her womb? yea, they may forget, yet will I not forget thee" (Isaiah 49:15). He that keeps Israel "shall neither slumber nor sleep" (Psalm 121:4). He has His plan and He is working it out.

It is important to remember that there is basically only one way of salvation both in Old Testament times and in New Testament times. It is only through the sacrifice of Christ the Lamb of God that any sinner can be saved or ever could be saved. There is only one covenant of grace and, although the administration of that covenant in the Old Testament was somewhat different, yet essentially sinners are saved in the same way. The one condition of the covenant of grace is faith. People are required to repent and believe the gospel. Men and women needed to be born again in Old Testament times just as in the New. None was saved by keeping the law or performing ritual. Paul tells the Roman Christians: "By the deeds of the law there shall no flesh be justified in his sight: for by the law is the knowledge of sin" (Romans 3:20). The law can only show us our sins and condemn us. In this sense it is our schoolmaster driving us to Christ as the only hope for guilty sinners (Galatians 3:24). The church of God in the Old Testament and in the New Testament are one, composed of elect sinners who have put their faith in Christ and are saved by grace. Stephen reminds us of this when he names God's people journeying from Egypt to the promised land as "the church in the wilderness" (Acts 7:38).

Zechariah's day was something like our own. It was discouraging times for the people of God. The church was very weak and in a depressed condition. Judah had been in captivity in Babylon for 70 years but in 539BC Cyrus the leader of the Medes and Persians conquered Babylon. The following year, as the new emperor, he decreed that the Jews could return to their own land and build the temple again. Many had prospered and were comfortably settled where they were, so that only a relatively small number chose to return. Very soon the altar of the Lord was set up again in Jerusalem and the public worship of God resumed. They began rebuilding the temple, but it was a big job. They were few in number and their resources were small. They faced opposition from the people who lived round about them, especially the Samaritans. The Jews were soon discouraged and gave up the work of building the temple. They were more concerned to build and beautify their own homes and develop their own lands.

Twenty years later, on the first day of the sixth month in the second year of the emperor Darius, 519BC, God addressed them through the prophet Haggai. He said, "This people say, The time is not come, the time that the Lord's house should be built" (Haggai 1:2). How often we procrastinate! We know what we should do but we say, "Not yet." We say, "I will do it later when I have more time." God challenges the Jewish church with strong words in verse 4, "Is it time for you, O ye, to dwell in your cieled houses, and this house lie waste?" (Haggai 1:4). They were living in beautiful cieled or panelled homes while the temple of the Lord was a heap of stones. God calls to them, "Consider your ways. Ye have sown much, and bring in little; ye eat, but ye have not enough; ye drink, but ye are not filled with drink; ye clothe you, but there is none warm; and he that earneth wages earneth wages to put it into a bag with holes" (vv5-6). These are powerful words. The Jews were not enjoying God's blessing. Instead of prospering economically their harvests were small. When they earned money and put it in their purses, these purses seemed to have a hole in the bottom. Money just disappeared and no matter how hard they worked they were not getting richer but rather poorer. Thankfully they listened to the word of the Lord and on the 24th day of that month, the sixth month, they returned to building the house of God.

Two months later the word of the Lord came to Zechariah. Just like Haggai he had been given a ministry of encouraging the building of the house of God, the temple. It took another four years for the temple to be built. Their financial resources in the days of Haggai and Zechariah were very limited in comparison to that of Solomon. They were few in number. It was easy for them to be discouraged but God said to them through Haggai, "The silver is mine, and the gold is mine, saith the Lord of hosts. The glory of this latter house shall be greater than of the former, saith the Lord of hosts: and in this place will I give peace, saith the Lord of hosts" (Haggai 2:8-9). The glory of the second temple would be greater than the first because the "Desire of all nations" (Haggai 2:7), the Messiah, would come and preach in this very temple and fill it with His glory.

Now Zechariah joins Haggai in this ministry of encouragement, but he also goes further. He is given visions which reveal so much more. He has a great deal to say not just to the Jews of 519BC but also to us today. Studying these visions will make us optimistic Christians who will labour for the Lord in our day looking for the spread of the gospel through the world, the conversion of the Jews to Christ, and, following that, the promised life from the dead coming to the Gentile church of which Paul speaks (Romans 11:15). It will not be the mere work of man. God will do it. The spiritual temple, the New Jerusalem, will be built, "Not by might nor by power, but by my Spirit, saith the Lord of hosts" (Zechariah 4:6). Christ shall rule the nations with a rod of iron and all shall bow before him: "All kings shall fall down before Him: all nations shall serve Him" (Psalm 72:11).

So then, let us now consider the introduction to the visions and, indeed, to this whole book.

1. God Speaks (v1)

"In the eighth month, in the second year of Darius, came the word of the Lord unto Zechariah, the son of Berechiah, the son of Iddo the prophet, saying..."

Here in verse 1 we are told of the coming of the "word of the Lord unto Zechariah." What we have in the book of Zechariah, as in all Scripture, is not the mere dreams, imagination and reflections of a prophet. It is divine revelation. Many today, even in the leadership of churches, think of the Bible as simply a human product. No, as we see here in verse 1, it is "the word of the Lord" that came to Zechariah. Peter tells us, "For the prophecy came not in old time by the will of man: but holy men of God spake as they were moved by the Holy Ghost" (2 Peter 1:21). These prophets were carried along by the Spirit of God so that what they wrote is the actual word of God. It is vitally important to grasp this. All other religions are the mere reflections of men. They imagine what God is like and what God requires. However, in the Bible, the true God really does speak.

Paul explains what we have in the Bible. He states: "All scripture is given by inspiration of God, and is profitable for doctrine, for reproof, for correction, for instruction in righteousness: that the man of God may be perfect, thoroughly furnished unto all good works" (2 Timothy 3:16-17). Inspiration means that all Scripture is, literally, God-breathed. God breathes out every word. What we have here, is not the thoughts of Zechariah but a message from God. It was addressed to the people in Jerusalem in 519BC but it is also addressed to us today. It is a divine revelation to us. Further, all of it is profitable for us too. It teaches, rebukes, corrects, and instructs us. Jesus often said, "He that hath ears to hear let him hear." For Him, "It is written..." (Matthew 4:4) was the same as "God said" and came with all the authority of God and was therefore final. Christ accepted the authority of Scripture and so should we. Jesus asserted, "The scripture cannot be broken" (John 10:35). It will stand forever. The Bible is the word of God and it is infallible and inerrant.

God still speaks to us today, but He does it through the Scriptures. His Spirit illuminates our hearts. He impresses the truth upon our minds. Everything we need to know for our salvation is there in the Bible. It declares to us as the *Westminster Shorter Catechism* states in the answer to Question 3: "What man is to believe concerning God, and what duty God requires of man." We are to treat the Bible with all the respect which is due to God. It calls upon us to repent of our sins, believe in Jesus Christ as our Saviour and so to escape the coming wrath of God which will descend without mercy upon all who persist in unbelief. We must obey and flee from the wrath to come to the Lord Jesus Christ. Also, in connection with faithful preaching of the gospel, we must remember what Jesus said to His followers, "He that heareth you heareth me; and he that despiseth you despiseth me; and he that despiseth me despiseth him that sent me" (Luke 10:16). When the preacher preaches the word of the Lord today, it must be listened to as if it was spoken by God Himself. So first of all then, in verse 1 we notice that the God of heaven is speaking and we must pay attention.

2. God was displeased with your fathers (v2)

"The Lord hath been sore displeased with your fathers."

In verse 2 we see that God was very angry with their fathers. This is rather obvious. Everywhere there are the charred remains of destroyed houses. The walls of Jerusalem are broken down, her palaces burnt and her temple in ruins. The land is a wilderness. Thorns and thistles have taken over.

The old prophets had warned of the coming judgment if the people would not repent. But they had been ignored. However, their words were not empty threats. Jeremiah told the Jews that they would spend 70 years in Babylon and his words were fulfilled. God saw the idolatry, the immorality, the Sabbath breaking and the oppression. He is a holy God and He hates sin. He wants His people to be a holy people, to love and obey Him. They show that they really love Him by keeping His commandments. Disobedience is the result of a lack of love for God.

It is the same today. We are grieved that the church is so weak. Here in Britain, relative to past years, few attend church. Many large church buildings lie derelict. Others are used as warehouses. Some have been transformed into public houses and night clubs. Some have been converted into flats. Not so long ago most people went to church. Christianity in the past was respected and honoured by society. Today, sadly, it is despised. The church of God is forsaken. The only churches which appear to grow are those which provide worldly music and entertainment. The world has invaded and taken over these churches. The worship is not for the glory of God but for the pleasure of man. God has withdrawn Himself from our churches. There is no power with the preaching of the word. Few are truly being born again. The church it seems has been forsaken by God. It has been left to die. It is in ruins.

Do you feel this? Are you troubled at the low state of the church? Is it a burden to you? Are you concerned for the future of the church?

3. Turn unto me (v3)

"Therefore say thou unto them, Thus saith the Lord of hosts; Turn ye unto me, saith the Lord of hosts."

Here in verse 3 we have a great call from God: "Turn ye unto me, saith the Lord of hosts." Essentially, God is saying to the Jews that they are on the wrong road. They are like lost sheep. They are going away from God. They are in a state of rebellion from Him. They are like sheep going astray, turning everyone to his own way. They are pleasing themselves instead of God. They are backsliding from Him. Sadly, this problem continued at that time among the Jews. The exact same message is proclaimed in the last book of the Old Testament, the prophecy of Malachi, which was written around seventy years later, "Return unto me, and I will return unto you, saith the Lord of Hosts" (Malachi 3:7).

Is this not a highly relevant message for us today also? The fear of God seems to have disappeared from our country and even from our churches. There is no reverence for God. There is little love for Him. We have become lovers of pleasures rather than lovers of God. We are far too much taken up with our jobs, our families, our homes, our friends and our entertainments. God is not central in our hearts and lives. There is a huge amount of hypocrisy around. We draw near to God with our lips while our hearts are far from Him (Matthew 15:18). We say we are Christians but are not as earnest and sincere as we should be. We pretend to be good real Christians but it is all so superficial. We forget that the eye of God is upon us. God does not judge by the outward appearance. He sees our hearts. He is aware of our thoughts. He sees the rottenness inside us.

So here there is a call to repent. The Jews were to return to the Lord. We, too, need to return to God. Search your heart. Consider your ways. Measure yourself in the light of God's Word. Examine yourself by the law of God and its searching demands. Think of Calvary and all that Christ suffered for our sins. See the wonderful love of Christ. Remember it was your sins that nailed Him to the tree. How horrible sin is!

Turn unto me, says God. Repent of your sins. Hate your sins. Turn from them in sorrow. Grieve over how you have failed to serve God. Let the love of Christ constrain you to new obedience. Take Christ as your Master. Show your love for Him by your repentance. Seek His grace to help you. Some think of repentance as something they do only at the point when they are converted, at the beginning of their Christian life. Actually, repentance is something we should be doing every day. Every day we are to be repenting of our sins and believing in Jesus afresh.

4. A Promise (v3)

"I will turn unto you, saith the Lord of hosts."

Here in verse 3 a promise is made: "Turn unto me saith the Lord of hosts, and I will turn unto you." It is a great promise. We want God's presence and blessing. We want God to be with us. Why did the exile take place? It was because God had left them. And when God left them, they were unable to fight successfully against their enemies. Like Samson without his hair, they were weak and like other men. When God was with them one could chase a thousand and two put ten thousand to flight (Deuteronomy 32:30).

Now they have returned to Judah. God has been gracious to them. They are allowed back to their own land again. But it seems that they have not learned the lessons of the exile. God has chastened them but they have ignored His rod of discipline.

It is true that they are no longer worshipping Baal. They have given up their physical idols but they have made gods for themselves out of their families, their homes, their fields and their money. Instead of concentrating on God and serving Him and building His temple they have been busy with their own houses, farms, businesses, and pleasures. But they are earning money to put it in a bag with holes. Their money is disappearing as fast as they earn it. There is no blessing in their labours. Further their enemies are threatening them on every side.

When God was with Israel the Egyptians could not hold them in slavery. The army of Egypt which came against them was drowned in the Red Sea. When God was with them the walls of Jericho fell down flat before them. All they had to do was walk round the city seven days, blow their trumpets and shout. With God's help young David could overcome the mighty giant Goliath, just with a sling and a stone.

Today the church is weak and despised. It has no power. It has few genuine converts. But here is a great promise. Turn unto me and I will turn to you. God will return. If only we would repent, then we would be greatly blessed. How different things would be if God returned! Try to see this for yourself. Prove Him and you will see how He keeps his promises.

5. Do not be like your fathers (v4)

"Be ye not as your fathers, unto whom the former prophets have cried, saying, Thus saith the Lord of hosts; Turn ye now from your evil ways, and from your evil doings: but they did not hear, nor hearken unto me, saith the Lord."

In verse 4 we read: "Be ye not as your fathers, unto whom the former prophets cried." The old prophets called your fathers to repent but they refused. Your fathers ignored the prophets and continued in their sins. They came to Jeremiah asking him for a word from God. They said they would obey God whatever He said. But when Jeremiah gave them the word from God they refused to obey. They had made up their own mind (Jeremiah 42). Their fathers came to listen to Ezekiel. But they treated him as an entertainer. He was to them as a musician. His words tickled their ears. Again, they listened but they did not obey (Ezekiel 33:31-33).

You and I must not be like our fathers. No doubt we today suffer for the sins of our fathers. It is at least partially because of their sins that we are afflicted and weak. God was grieved at their sins, their outward profession of faith but inner lust. Their hypocrisy angered God. He saw their pride, greed, envy, strife and immorality. He noted their failure to train their children in His ways. He noted the respect they gave to the liberal scholars who denied the full inspiration of Scripture. They let clever unbelieving men take over the theological colleges and train men for the ministry. But they trained them in doubting the Bible and undermining the full gospel. Learn from the sins of your fathers. Do not copy them.

6. Your fathers are gone (v5)

"Your fathers, where are they? and the prophets, do they live for ever?"

Here in verse 5 the prophet asks where their fathers are. These fathers ignored the warnings of the prophets and so judgment came upon them and they are gone. The sword took some of them away. Famine and disease in the siege of Jerusalem led to the death of many others. Those who were left were carried away into captivity. The wages of sin is death (Romans 6:23).

GOD SPEAKS

Our fathers have died too. They allowed liberalism into the pulpits and worldliness into the pews. Doubt was cast on the word of God. Ministers were allowed to criticise the truth, deny creation and reject the substitutionary atonement of Christ and still remain as ministers. Instead of following the directions of Scripture regarding worship – the regulative principle of worship – they changed the worship into that which is pleasing to man. Churches became "seeker-sensitive" rather than God-sensitive. Their concern was to offend no one but the result was that they offended God. Our fathers have now gone to meet the Judge and to render their account.

The prophets who warned them are gone too. The faithful preachers who stood against the tide of unbelief which was coming in have passed on. Those godly men who warned of the spiritual danger the church was in have now gone to their reward. They warned against sin but were ignored and despised. Life is short. A day of reckoning is coming.

7. God's Word remains (v6)

"But my words and my statutes, which I commanded my servants the prophets, did they not take hold of your fathers? and they returned and said, Like as the Lord of hosts thought to do unto us, according to our ways, and according to our doings, so hath he dealt with us."

Verse 6 makes it all plain: "Like as the Lord of hosts thought to do unto us, according to our ways and according to our doings, so hath he dealt with us." God's word is true and has been proved so time and again. Every word of God will stand. The Scriptures cannot be broken. The Jews hated Jeremiah and ridiculed him but they have to admit now that all he said was true and came to pass. They thought that Jerusalem would never be destroyed. They felt sure that God would never allow his temple to be burnt. But it happened just as Jeremiah and the other prophets had warned.

God's threats are not empty words. We must listen to what he says. Turn back to God. Put away your idols. Humble yourself before him.

Cleanse your hands you sinners and purify your hearts you double minded (James 4:8). Return unto the Lord and He will return unto you.

Today I warn you from God. Remember what happened to the ancient world. For 120 years Noah was a preacher of righteousness calling sinners to repent, but the people of his day would not listen. The ark was built but they would not enter into it. They carried on with their godless lives. Then the flood came and destroyed them. It was too late when they went and knocked on the door of the ark. God had shut the door and no man could open it. When Lot warned his sons-in-law of the coming fire and brimstone, he seemed to them as one that mocked. It all appeared as a joke. But the fire came the next morning and destroyed them (Genesis 19:12-29).

Jesus was told of the tower of Siloam falling on 18 people and killing them. He warned the people: Do you think those on whom the tower fell were greater sinners than others? No, He said, but unless you repent you shall all likewise perish (Luke 13:5). Whatever we witness of accidents and tragedies should be seen as coming from God. It is not that those who suffered were greater sinners than those who did not. Rather, we all deserve to suffer and if we do not repent we will suffer something far worse. We will suffer an eternity in hell.

Are you unsaved today? If you are, you are in a dangerous position. How important it is for you to repent! This world is doomed. Hell is real. Make your peace with God. Turn from your sins and trust in Jesus. Flee from the wrath to come and cast yourself on Christ for mercy.

Fellow Christians, let each one of us repent of our own personal sins. Let us turn back to God. He has promised to turn back to us. If we repent we will experience His blessing. We as individuals need God with us.

As churches let us examine our ways in the light of Scripture. Let us return to the Lord. Let us repent of our sins. Let us maintain high standards of holiness in our churches. Let us teach the whole Word of God. Let us practise proper, biblical church discipline. Let us worship God exactly as He has laid down for us in the Scriptures. We long for revival. If we will repent, the Lord has promised to return to us.

CHAPTER 2

FIRST VISION: THE MAN ON THE RED HORSE

(Zechariah 1:7-17)

In this second section of the prophecy we are dealing with the first of Zechariah's visions. We are living in discouraging times for the church in Britain and in the West generally. Congregations tend to be small and elderly. We see little success in evangelism. There are few conversions. Secularism has taken over our culture. At one time the Bible, the Ten Commandments, and the Gospel were taught in our schools, but that is no longer the case. Now every false religion is given priority over the truth. Sexual immorality is promoted through sex education. Gender confusion is encouraged and the divine institution of marriage is undermined. The theory of evolution is promoted as scientific fact. In society generally the Sabbath as God's holy day of rest is disregarded. Unborn children are murdered in their millions in their mothers' wombs and it is regarded as the mother's right to choose to kill. God's name is blasphemed and used as a swear word. Christian values are despised in the media. There is no fear of God in society. Few, even in the churches, believe in the wrath of God and hell. Most people are spiritually apathetic and give no thought to God, death, judgment and eternity. The only growing churches are Charismatic ones in which there is worldly music, fake miracles, excitement, and entertainment and little reverence for God. It seems as if God has forsaken us. There is little real, serious, felt Christianity. But here in the prophecy of Zechariah we find great encouragement. This prophet also lived in dark days. God gives him these eight visions to strengthen his faith and that of his fellow-countrymen. Instead of focussing on Jerusalem in ruins he is encouraged to look up! And we too must lift up our eyes from the spiritual desolations around us and realise that God is on the throne. He is reigning and working out His purposes. Look and see the man on the red horse.

1. The Man in the Myrtle Trees (vv7-8)

"Upon the four and twentieth day of the eleventh month, which is the month Sebat, in the second year of Darius, came the word of the Lord unto Zechariah, the son of Berechiah, the son of Iddo the prophet, saying, I saw by night, and behold a man riding upon a red horse, and he stood among the myrtle trees that were in the bottom; and behind him were there red horses, speckled, and white."

Some three months after the first revelation with which we dealt in the first chapter a new revelation is given to the prophet. This time the Lord uses a vision rather than simply words. Zechariah sees myrtle trees in the bottom of the valley. Cyrus, the emperor, had allowed the Jews to return from their exile in Babylon. They came to Jerusalem and set up the altar of the Lord and begun building the temple. But soon they became discouraged and a further twenty years passed with no progress. Then the word of the Lord came to Haggai and he began prophesying on the first day of the sixth month of the second year of the emperor Darius, i.e., two months before the first revelation to Zechariah. Haggai challenged the Jews to start working again on the temple and they responded by returning again to the work. Shortly after that Zechariah joined Haggai in encouraging the builders in their work on the temple. We noticed in our previous chapter the promise he gave from the Lord, "Turn ye unto me saith the Lord of hosts and I will turn unto you, saith the Lord of hosts" (Zechariah 1:3). Now, exactly five months after the work began, Zechariah is given a new encouraging vision on the 24th day of the 11th month of the second year of Darius.

The prophet sees a man on a red horse among the myrtle trees in the valley. These trees are a picture of the church. They are not tall cedars nor are they mighty oaks. Myrtle trees reach only a maximum height of three metres. They are mere bushy trees and nothing special to look at. God's people are not impressive to look at. Their leaves are a dark, shiny green and when crushed give a pleasant fragrance. God's people when bruised turn to the Lord in prayer and their prayers are as incense poured forth. Notice also that the trees are not on the mountain top but in the valley, in a lowly place. Often God's people are in a low condition. But in the middle of them is the man on the red horse. Who is He? Verse 11 makes plain that He is the angel of the Lord. Always in the Old Testament the angel of the Lord is the Lord Jesus Himself. It is the Son of God appearing in human form. For example, when God required Abraham to offer up Isaac and he had bound his son upon the altar and had raised the knife to kill his son, the angel of the Lord who is identified as God himself called to him from heaven to stop him (Genesis 22:11-12). Similarly, the angel of the Lord appeared to Manoah and his wife in Judges 13 and they recognised Him as God. The church is poor, weak, and afflicted, yet wonderfully the Lord Himself is in the midst.

We find something similar when God appears to Moses in the desert calling him to lead Israel out of the land of Egypt. We are told that Moses saw a bush burning with fire and yet the bush was not consumed. When he drew near to observe this strange phenomenon, God called to him out of the midst of the bush, "Draw not nigh hither: put off thy shoes from off thy feet, for the place whereon thou standest is holy ground. Moreover he said, I am the God of thy father, the God of Abraham, the God of Isaac, and the God of Jacob. And Moses hid his face; for he was afraid to look upon God" (Exodus 3:5-6). The bush that was not consumed represents the church of God, and God Himself dwells in the bush. Because God's people are sinful you would expect the bush to be burnt but miraculously the bush is spared. God's people are afflicted yet are precious to Him and so they are spared. They have a great Saviour who atoned for their sins. Christ's blood cleanses from all sin. The burning bush which is an emblem used by the presbyterian churches encourages us to trust in our God who dwells in His church, and although they are sinners, He does not consume them. He loves His blood-bought people and cares deeply for them. Behind the man riding upon the red horse the prophet sees others, "red horses, speckled, and white" (v8).

2. The Lord is in control (vv9-10)

"Then said I, O my lord, what are these? And the angel that talked with me said unto me, I will shew thee what these be. And the man that stood among the myrtle trees answered and said, These are they whom the Lord hath sent to walk to and fro through the earth."

Zechariah asks, "What are these?" It is explained: "And the man that stood among the myrtle trees answered and said, These are they whom the Lord hath sent to walk to and fro through the earth" (v10). The Persian emperors had messengers or inspectors whom they sent out to the various provinces under their rule to keep them informed and bring them back word of the state of affairs in these various provinces. They would inform the emperor of unrest or signs of rebellion or any problems developing. What we have here are angels sent out to report back to heaven how things were going on earth. God knows everything that is happening on the earth but it is told this human way for our benefit. We find something like this in the book of Job: "Now there was a day when the sons of God came to present themselves before the Lord, and Satan came also among them. And the Lord said unto Satan, Whence comest thou? Then Satan answered the Lord, and said, From going to and fro in the earth, and from walking up and down in it" (Job 1:6-7). The sons of God here are obviously the angels. Satan is among them as he was originally an angel. He and the angels had been going to and fro though the earth seeing what was going on. God asked him, "Hast thou considered my servant Job, that there is none like him in the earth, a perfect and an upright man, one that feareth God, and escheweth evil?" (Job 1:8).

3. An Angelic Report (v11)

"And they answered the angel of the Lord that stood among the myrtle trees, and said, We have walked to and fro through the earth, and, behold, all the earth sitteth still, and is at rest."

We have here the angels reporting back to the Lord. They have surveyed the earth. They have gone into even the remotest nations. They know exactly what is going on in the earth and they report that, "All the earth sitteth still, and is at rest." At this time there was peace and prosperity in the Persian empire. The earth sat still and there was no war. People were prospering materially. Yet the Lord's people were afflicted, downtrodden and depressed. The colour of the horses as in Revelation chapter 6 point to war, famine, disease, and death.

Is it not the same in our world today? Many people are prosperous. They are eating and drinking and making merry. They have their entertainments, their pleasures, and their holidays. Most of the world is enjoying peace. Life is easy. They have no cares or worries. People talk of inflation, the increased cost of the weekly shopping, the rise in the price of fuel for heating and transport, yet the roads are full of cars and the airports crowded with holiday-makers. But what about the people of God? They are everywhere despised, mocked and ridiculed. In many countries they are actively persecuted. Many Christians are in prison for their faith. Others live in constant fear. Thousands die as martyrs every year in countries like North Korea, Afghanistan, and Nigeria. Yet God is over all and in control.

4. A Powerful Intercession (v12)

"Then the angel of the Lord answered and said, O Lord of hosts, how long wilt thou not have mercy on Jerusalem and on the cities of Judah, against which thou hast had indignation these threescore and ten years?"

Again, we remember that the angel of the Lord is the Lord Jesus Christ, the second person of the Trinity appearing in human form. As one of the Puritans put it: He appeared in the Old Testament trying on as it were the clothes of human nature which He would later assume forever at His incarnation. Notice the strong intercession of our Mediator: "Then the angel of the Lord answered and said, O Lord of hosts, how long wilt thou not have mercy on Jerusalem and on the cities of Judah, against which thou hast had indignation these threescore and ten years?" (v12). Christ is praying for His church. It is seventy years since the temple was destroyed by Nebuchadnezzar and his Chaldean army. Surely it is time for God's wrath to cease. Has He not punished His beloved people enough?

But if the one speaking here is God, the Second Person, how can He pray to God? Surely God cannot pray to Himself. True, God does not and cannot pray to Himself because God is one and there is only one divine will in God. But as a man Christ could pray and certainly did pray. God cannot suffer and die. Yet He became a man in order to suffer and die for us. He could not be our Saviour without His incarnation. He became a man, a true and real man, to pray and to intercede for us. He is our Prophet, Priest and King as a man. As a man He is our Mediator. While it is true that He only became a man five hundred years after Zechariah yet His saving work and His mediatorial work stretched back into Old Testament times. Also, in this same sense He is the "Lamb slain from the foundation of the world" (Revelation 13:8). The Lamb did not die till 2000 years ago but it was so sure that Christ would die that it is put this way. Old Testament believers trusted in the finished work of Christ, and were saved by it, though in their day the work was not yet begun. Further, we must remember that God is eternal and not subject to time as we are. He is above time. He has no past nor future.

So here we have Christ praying for His church in the days of Zechariah. Who can pray as effectively as our Lord? We are encouraged when someone says they are praying for us, but surely there is no one who could pray for us as effectively as our Saviour. Christ loves us and pleads for us. Even when we sin He still cares and prays for us: "My little children, these things write I unto you, that ye sin not. And if any man sin, we have an advocate with the Father, Jesus Christ the righteous: And he is the propitiation for our sins: and not for ours only, but also for the sins of the whole world" (1 John 2:1-2). Christ is praying for His own.

The Jews were sad because of these seventy years during which the temple was in ruins but now there is a mighty one praying for them. The past seventy years in the UK and in the West has seen a catastrophic decline in the church. There has been no general revival of the church since 1860 and in the recent past there has been a wholesale forsaking of the church.

Secularism has taken over. Immorality has reached new levels never before seen in the history of the world. The grossest filthiness is practised and boasted of, for example in Gay Pride marches. Man, generally, believes that the world came into existence by means of the 'Big Bang' and the theory of evolution. There is in their eyes no God, nor need for God. There is no afterlife. Man has made a god of himself and zealously worships that god. Is there a future for the church? How long O Lord! But it is wonderfully encouraging to know that the Son of God is interceding for the church. Join the Lord Jesus in praying the prayer we have here which the Father will certainly answer.

5. A Comforting Message (v13)

"And the Lord answered the angel that talked with me with good words and comfortable words."

We notice here the response God gives to the Angel's intercession. The Lord answered with good and comfortable words. They were dark days, yet there is this encouraging message. No matter how discouraging the situation God is in control. He is working out His purposes. God loves His people and cares for them. He will ensure that none of them is lost. His church has a great future.

6. God Jealous for His people (vv14-15)

"So the angel that communed with me said unto me, Cry thou, saying, Thus saith the Lord of hosts; I am jealous for Jerusalem and for Zion with a great jealousy. And I am very sore displeased with the heathen that are at ease: for I was but a little displeased, and they helped forward the affliction."

The prophet is given instructions that he should cry out and tell the Jews that the Lord of hosts is jealous for Jerusalem and for Zion with a great jealousy (v14). We generally take the word "jealous" in a negative sense. We rightly see it as a sin to be jealous of someone else. But here it is used in a good sense. It refers to the very strong love of a faithful husband for his wife. God has a deep concern for His bride, the church. He has a deep personal interest in her and a terrible anger towards those who would abuse His wife. Zion is precious to Him and He will fight those who hurt her.

Now, God says that He is "very sore displeased with the heathen that are at ease." They show no concern for the suffering church of God. Further God states that He "was but a little displeased, and they helped forward the affliction" (v15). Yes, God was angry with His people because of their idolatry, but it was a little anger. He was but a little displeased. But when He chastised His people the heathen jumped in as it were and added to the pain inflicted on Zion. They kicked Israel when she was down. God now feels sorry for His people. He will unleash his full anger against the heathen. The instrument which He used to chastise His chosen, will now be punished with His full wrath.

In verse 11 we had noted the report of the angels that "all the earth sitteth still, and is at rest." The Persians and the other nations are at ease. This cannot be allowed. God will now punish them. God had said through Haggai, "Yet once, it is a little while, and I will shake the heavens, and the earth, and the sea, and the dry land; And I will shake all nations, and the desire of all nations shall come: and I will fill this house with glory, saith the Lord of hosts" (Haggai 2:6-7). God shook the nations and raised up the Greeks led by Alexander the Great to conquer the Persians. And then God again shook the nations raising up the empire of Rome. Eventually the Christ, "the desire of all nations" (Haggai 2:7), came. Later Antichrist will arise but he will be destroyed. The author of the Epistle to the Hebrews writes: "See that ye refuse not him that speaketh. For if they escaped not who refused him that spake on earth, much more shall not we escape, if we turn away from him that speaketh from heaven: Whose voice then shook the earth: but now he hath promised, saying, Yet once more I shake not the earth only, but also heaven. And this word, Yet once more, signifieth the removing of those things that are shaken, as of things that are made, that those things which cannot be shaken may remain. Wherefore we receiving a kingdom which cannot be moved, let us have grace, whereby we may serve God acceptably with reverence and godly fear: For our God is a consuming fire" (Hebrew 12:25-29).

The wicked despise and mock the people of God. They are allowed for a time to trample upon the saints, but then God will arise in His wrath and destroy these enemies of His beloved. Atheists, heretics, followers of false religions and all the ungodly will experience His indignation. Notice how it is stated in the Psalms: "Why do the heathen rage, and the people imagine a vain thing? The kings of the earth set themselves, and the rulers take counsel together, against the Lord, and against his anointed, saying, Let us break their bands asunder, and cast away their cords from us. He that sitteth in the heavens shall laugh: the Lord shall have them in derision. Then shall he speak unto them in his wrath, and vex them in his sore displeasure" (Psalm 2:1-5). Make sure you are not an enemy of God's people! What hope is there for you if God will turn on you in His infinite wrath?

7. A Wonderful Promise (v16-17)

"Therefore thus saith the Lord; I am returned to Jerusalem with mercies: my house shall be built in it, saith the Lord of hosts, and a line shall be stretched forth upon Jerusalem. Cry yet, saying, Thus saith the Lord of hosts; My cities through prosperity shall yet be spread abroad; and the Lord shall yet comfort Zion, and shall yet choose Jerusalem."

Verse 16 tells us that God loves his people and will return to them. The work of building the temple will be completed. God had turned His back on the Jews because He was displeased and grieved at their sins, but now He returns to them and assures them of His help. They had many enemies trying to stop the work. Though they had limited resources and they were few in number, yet the house of the Lord would be built again. It took another four years, but the word of the Lord was fulfilled.

Furthermore, there were to be better days ahead. A line, a surveyor's line, would be stretched over Jerusalem. Houses, many houses, would be built. The next verse explains more fully: "Cry yet, saying, Thus saith the Lord of hosts; My cities through prosperity shall yet be spread abroad; and the Lord shall yet comfort Zion, and shall yet choose Jerusalem" (v17).

The prophet is urged to cry aloud. Here is a wonderful encouraging message for the builders of the temple. It comes from the Lord of hosts. He is the God of the armies of heaven. He is almighty. With Him all things are possible. Not just Jerusalem will expand, but also the other cities of Judah will increase and grow. Through prosperity they shall spread abroad. God is comforting His people. He shall yet choose Jerusalem and cause his name to be there. Shout out this encouragement!

God did indeed cause Jerusalem to be built. It happened literally for the Jews. The temple was completed. Seventy years later in the days of Nehemiah the walls of Jerusalem were built again. The Jews multiplied and prospered. Many thousands came to live in the city. God chose Jerusalem. The Son of God became man, born in Bethlehem, near Jerusalem. Later, He entered the temple and taught there. Rejected by the chief priests and elders He was handed over to the Romans and crucified outside the walls of Jerusalem. But then on the third day He rose again. He ascended up to heaven from the Mount of Olives and sat on the right hand of God. He sent His Spirit to His people in Jerusalem on the day of Pentecost. Three thousand Jews were converted that day. The numbers in His church quickly multiplied. Later Gentiles were also born again by the Spirit of God. From this beginning the New Jerusalem grew. It expanded rapidly across the known world. Today millions from every nation are to be found in this church of God.

To Nebuchadnezzar and Daniel it had been revealed that God's kingdom would be like a little stone cut without human hands out of a mountain. It would strike the image which represents the earthly empires and destroy them and would then grow till it became a mountain which filled the earth (Daniel 2). Jesus told many parables which described the growth of His kingdom and church. For example, He spoke of the little mustard seed, "Which indeed is the least of all seeds: but when it is grown, it is the greatest among herbs, and becometh a tree, so that the birds of the air come and lodge in the branches thereof" (Matthew 13:32). Then He told of the leaven, "The kingdom of heaven is like unto leaven, which a woman took, and hid in three measures of meal, till the whole was leavened" (v33). These parables make plain that God's church will spread through the whole world and become a mighty kingdom. Further we are told that "God sent not his Son into the world to condemn the world; but that the world through him might be saved" (John 3:17). This verse implies that in a very real sense the world shall be saved. It is not simply a remnant that will be saved, plucked as it were from a perishing world. Rather, so many will be saved that it can be said that the world will be saved. Christ's work will be eminently successful. In all things He shall have the pre-eminence (Colossians 1:18).

There were and will be set-backs. There will be dark days but the future prosperity of the church is guaranteed. She shall spread abroad. The Lord has chosen Jerusalem. Do not let the devil discourage you, if you are on the side of Christ, you are on the side of victory. And even the literal Jerusalem shall yet be chosen by God. For many years it was a deserted city. It is now the capital again of a Jewish state. But Paul assures us that the Jews, who have for so long been rejected by God, will yet again be grafted in to their own olive tree, "For the gifts and calling of God are without repentance" (Romans 11:29). The Psalmist foretells concerning the Messiah: "He shall have dominion also from sea to sea, and from the river unto the ends of the earth. They that dwell in the wilderness shall bow before him; and his enemies shall lick the dust. The kings of Tarshish and of the isles shall bring presents: the kings of Sheba and Seba shall offer gifts. Yea, all kings shall fall down before him: all nations shall serve him" (Psalm 72:8-11).

CHAPTER 3

SECOND VISION: THE FOUR HORNS

(Zechariah 1:18-21)

God's people have many enemies. Sometimes we feel beaten and battered and our head hangs down. Should we be angry with God for allowing this situation to develop? Should we allow hatred in our hearts towards our enemies? Jesus taught us to love our enemies. We are to lift up our eyes and see that the Lord reigns. Nothing happens by chance. God is in control. He ensures that all things work together for our good. Here is a vision to encourage us in difficult times. The enemies of God's church will not prevail.

1. The Four Horns (vv18-19)

"Then lifted I up mine eyes, and saw, and behold four horns. And I said unto the angel that talked with me, What be these? And he answered me, These are the horns which have scattered Judah, Israel, and Jerusalem."

This vision is closely connected with the previous one. There it is said: "And I am very sore displeased with the heathen that are at ease: for I was but a little displeased, and they helped forward the affliction" (v15). These enemies opposed the Jews, but now God expresses His displeasure with them. The temple will be built. The church has a great future.

The prophet lifts up his eyes and sees four horns. He asks the angel which is showing him the visions what these are and what they are going to do. The angel replies: "These are the horns which have scattered Judah, so that no man did lift up his head: but these are come to fray them, to cast out the horns of the Gentiles, which lifted up their horn over the land of Judah to scatter it" (v21).

Horns are a symbol of power. We think of the horns of a ram or bull and how they fight and seek to assert their supremacy with their horns. We are not told what animals these horns belong to. It is a bit like the horses in the previous vision. We are told of the horses, but obviously their riders are included.

Why are four mentioned? This implies attack coming from the four points of the compass, north south, east, and west. From every side the Jews were being crushed. These horns symbolise the Philistines, the Moabites, the Edomites, the Ammonites, the Syrians, the Egyptians, the Samaritans and the Persians, indeed all their enemies. The Jews who were the people of God were bruised and battered and trampled underfoot. None of them could lift their heads. In the same way the church of God today is being attacked by enemies on every side. The enemies are powerful.

The church today is weak. The people of God feel oppressed and frightened. The four horns are very real. Attacks are directed against the church from every side. But what are the great enemies of the church today?

(1) *Evolutionary theory*
Where have we come from and where are we going have always been pressing questions for mankind. The church has provided the answers revealed by God in the Bible. However, the publication of Charles Darwin's *On the Origin of Species* in 1859 had a huge effect across the world. Up till this point people generally believed that God had created them and that one day they would die and must answer to God for their lives. But now the biblical account of creation was rejected by many. It seemed possible that life had begun by chance and the different forms arose from natural selection. People then began to question whether there is a God. The scientific community widely accepted evolution and came to promote it enthusiastically. Even many theologians and churches tried to accommodate Darwin's hypothesis. To begin with even some orthodox theologians were influenced. Also, geologists began to speak of an ancient earth. The Bible implies that the world is only a few thousand years old.

Many geologists now argued that the earth was thousands of millions of years old. If the first few chapters of Genesis cannot be trusted, can the rest of the Bible be trusted? More recently, Creation Scientists have shown how the Bible does not conflict with true science. The earth appears to be old but is not. The problems with evolution have been highlighted and the impossibility of life beginning by some kind of spontaneous generation demonstrated. But the schools, the universities, and the media all present evolution as a fact. Society generally has lost its fear of God because the majority do not want to believe in a Creator and Judge and they hope that science has explained God away. Evolution has been a huge horn by which the devil has attacked and continues to attack the church.

(2) *Liberal Theology*
Liberal theology came into prominence in Western Europe and America around the same time as the theory of evolution was popularised by Charles Darwin. It arose particularly in Germany where there were several famous old universities. Seeing the progress in science and other disciplines, theologians also wanted to come up with new discoveries. Higher criticism arose. Basically, this approach treated the Bible just like any other book and so, denying the Bible's supernatural character, these theologians cast doubt upon many of its statements. It meant that neither the history, nor the geography, nor even the theological and ethical statement could be trusted. Human reason became the judge of what was true and acceptable. Julius Wellhausen (1844-1918), for example, developed his Documentary Hypothesis reconstructing Old Testament history. He denied the Mosaic authorship of the Pentateuch and the whole historical account given in the first five books of the Bible. He argued that Deuteronomy was written in the time of king Josiah. Many theologians and ministers accepted his theories and they became very popular in the theological colleges. Some argued that it did not matter who wrote this book or that. Surely it was a minor point, they said, whether Moses wrote these books or not. Just take the teaching of the book, they argued. But it did matter. If the Bible itself said that it was written by Moses and if our

Lord Jesus said the same (for example Mark 10:3-5) then we must accept the Mosaic authorship or the authority of the Scriptures is undermined. If the Bible is wrong in the little things it states then it can be wrong in the major assertions it makes too. Sadly, this is what happened. The authority of Scripture was undermined. Human reason was instead placed on the throne. Soon even the substitutionary atonement of Christ was rejected. The idea of sacrifice and the blood of Christ and propitiation were seen as prescientific religion and unworthy of a God of love. Error always enters a little at a time. Once some of the statements of the Bible begin to be questioned, soon the other statements are questioned too. Sadly, this Liberalism has taken over all the mainline churches. Here we have another horn which batters the true church of God.

(3) *The Ecumenical Movement*

Over the last 100 years the importance of church unity has been stressed by such bodies as the World Council of Churches. Much is made of the fact that Jesus prayed for unity in His High Priestly prayer (John 17). Churches, they say, when united will surely be stronger. Doctrine is seen as divisive and so must be down-played. It is a kind of lowest common denominator kind of belief. Love is emphasised. We are told to forget our differences and worship together. The evangelical gospel is abandoned. Some churches teach salvation by good works and others salvation by taking the sacraments. The Liberalism of the mainline churches is predominant. The radical nature of the Christian gospel is forgotten and all religions are seen as different paths to God and salvation. Emphasis is laid on helping the poor but also on certain political concerns. The World Council of Churches used to be strongly against Apartheid while overlooking other evils. Today it tends to be pro-Palestinian and hostile to Israel. The Ecumenical Movement essentially empties the church of the gospel. The church becomes increasingly like a branch of the state, just involved in social work.

(4) *The Charismatic Movement*

Since the 1960s the Charismatic Movement has made huge inroads into the Christian church. Stress is laid on emotional excitement. Supernatural gifts such as tongue speaking, prophecy and healing are claimed by leaders. Many healings, when analysed, are simply the effect of mind over matter. The individual is convinced that he is healed when no actual healing has occurred. In other cases, there are fake healings. Where there is a failure to heal, the sufferer is blamed for a lack of faith. The music is worldly and the songs lack content. Words are repeated in a mindless emotionalism. One African theologian has compared it to the incantations of the witchdoctors. Evangelists in a callous way persuade people to part with their money promising them health and prosperity which of course never come. The prosperity preaching is widespread especially in the developing world and it does much damage. People become Christians because they have been promised health and wealth. But Christ promised His faithful followers tribulation in this world (John 16:33).

(5) *Sexual ethics*

There has been a remarkable transformation in sexual ethics in the last forty years. In the past everyone accepted that marriage should be between a man and a woman and that all sex outside marriage was wrong. Both premarital fornication and adultery within marriage were condemned. Homosexual practice was rightly seen as gross immorality. However today things have changed dramatically both in society and the churches. Sadly, too many churches receive their morality from the world around them. The world has invaded the church. Liberalism has undermined the authority of the Scriptures. Instead of viewing homosexuality as a sin it is argued that it is a condition that some people have from birth. The world says such people cannot help it or change it and therefore should embrace it. Mainline churches accept this and argue that love is love and must be good. But the Bible calls it not *love*, but *lust* (see, for example, Romans 1:27). Also, the Scriptures make plain that some are converted from that lifestyle and are in fact liberated from that bondage to sin. Paul wrote to the Corinthian church: "Be not deceived: neither fornicators, nor idolaters, nor adulterers, nor effeminate, nor abusers of themselves with mankind, nor thieves, nor covetous, nor drunkards, nor revilers, nor extortioners, shall inherit the kingdom of God. And such were some of you: but ye are washed, but ye are sanctified, but ye are justified in the name of the Lord Jesus, and by the Spirit of our God" (1 Corinthians 6:9-11; see also 1 Corinthians 5:11).

(6) *Postmodernism*
In recent times there has been the growth of the idea that religion should be private. People, it is said, should keep their beliefs to themselves. Postmodernism asserts that there is no such thing as absolute truth. Each person has their own truth. What you believe is right for you and what I believe is right for me. There must be no attempt to convert others. Evangelism is condemned. It is seen as totally wrong to challenge others or criticise their views. However true Christianity believes that there is such a thing as truth and that God is the source of truth. Those who believe the Bible have the truth. Evangelism is a vital element of healthy faith. Jesus stated quite clearly, "I am the way, the truth, and the life: no man cometh unto the Father, but by me" (John 14:6). All other religions lead to hell. All forms of the Christian faith which do not focus on Christ and Him crucified are heresy and destroy souls.

(7) *Worldliness*
People today have much more leisure-time than in ages past. Work does not absorb all their time and energy. There are many forms of entertainment readily available. TV, videos, YouTube, social media, etc. are a great temptation to many Christians. The time which used to be spent in studying the Scriptures, praying, reading Christian books and fellowshipping with other Christians is often now used for pleasure. People have become "lovers of pleasures more than lovers of God" (2 Timothy 3:4). The church has lost its zeal for holiness and for evangelism. God is grieved by the idolatry of church members who spend their time in trivial pursuits and fail to love Him with all their hearts.

(8) *Summary*

The church of God is being attacked from every side. The four horns batter it from north, south, east and west. How can it survive? Every true Christian knows what it is to fight against the world, the flesh and the devil. The church as a whole is surrounded on every side by enemies. Some of the enemies come softly and aim to seduce with wily cunning. Others attack head on with the great ferocity of persecutors. Christ said to his disciples, "I send you forth as sheep in the midst of wolves" (Matt.10:16). How can sheep possibly survive in the midst of a pack of wolves. Other attacks come from within, from wolves dressed up as sheep: "Beware of false prophets, which come to you in sheep's clothing, but inwardly they are ravening wolves" (Matthew 7:15). These can often be the hardest to resist because they are the most difficult to detect. Zechariah is told: "These are the horns which have scattered Judah, Israel, and Jerusalem." God's people are scattered by their enemies.

2. The Four Carpenters (vv20-21)

"And the Lord shewed me four carpenters. Then said I, What come these to do? And he spake, saying, These are the horns which have scattered Judah, so that no man did lift up his head: but these are come to fray them, to cast out the horns of the Gentiles, which lifted up their horn over the land of Judah to scatter it."

Zechariah then tells us that "The Lord showed me four carpenters." The prophet is curious: "What come these to do?" He was told, "These are the horns which have scattered Judah, so that no man did lift up his head: but these are come to fray them, to cast out the horns of the Gentiles, which lifted up their horn over the land of Judah to scatter it."

The horns seem all-powerful and the church in itself has no answer to them. But God does have an answer. He is Almighty. He loves His church. He chose it from eternity. He sent His Son to die for it. He has His plan. In His time and in His way, He will deliver His people. The horns of the Gentiles will not prevail. He sends the carpenters, or workmen, to cut and break them with saws and hammers.

Down through the centuries the heathen around Israel invaded their land time and again. The Chaldeans carried them away into captivity for seventy years. But even then the success of their enemies was limited. They were allowed to go so far and no further. They were instruments of chastisement in the hands of the Lord to correct His people. Eventually the Jews committed the great sin of rejecting and crucifying the Messiah. For this Jerusalem was destroyed and the Jews were scattered across the world. But the "gifts and calling of God are without repentance" (Romans 11:29). One day they will be restored and grafted again into the olive tree of the church. The horns of their enemies will be frayed and cast out.

The church today, as we have seen, has many powerful enemies arrayed against it. But God cares deeply for His church. The beloved people will not be destroyed. The horns of their enemies will be cut. There is no doubt about the future and success of God's church. They will tread down their enemies as the mire in the streets (Micah 7:10). Paul could say to the Roman church, "The God of peace shall bruise Satan under your feet shortly" (Romans 16:20). Even Satan will be overcome.

Rejoice Christian friends. You are on the victory side. The Lord will fight for you. "Be strong and of good courage" (Joshua 1:6). You will take possession of the land. As Paul said to the Romans: "Who shall separate us from the love of Christ? shall tribulation, or distress, or persecution, or famine, or nakedness, or peril, or sword? As it is written, For thy sake we are killed all the day long; we are accounted as sheep for the slaughter. Nay, in all these things we are more than conquerors through him that loved us" (Romans 8:35-37).

In these difficult days look up. God reigns. He sits on the throne above every throne. Remember the Son of God is the King and Head of the church. His enemies will be made His footstool (Hebrews 1:13). The true church is precious to Him because He purchased it with His own blood. He is interceding for it at God's right hand and His intercession is not in vain. Remember too that the Holy Spirit has come to live in the church. He is sanctifying it. He unites it to God. We have the promise, "Being confident of this very thing, that he which hath begun a good work in you will perform it until the day of Jesus Christ" (Philippians 1:6). He has said, "And they shall be mine, saith the Lord of hosts, in that day when I make up my jewels; and I will spare them, as a man spareth his own son that serveth him" (Malachi 3:17).

CHAPTER 4

THIRD VISION: THE MAN WITH THE MEASURING LINE

(Zechariah 2)

Christians in the twenty-first century, have a tendency to be pessimistic. For the past 150 years the church in Britain and Western Europe has been in decline. The church has continued to spread in Africa, South America and Asia, but it is generally very superficial and worldly. Most professing Christians show little zeal for the Lord. The Charismatic Movement with its emphasis on health and wealth, its superficial choruses, man-centred worship, absence of the fear of God and lack of emphasis on personal holiness, characterises the vast majority of Christians. Things seem to be going from bad to worse. Many of the best Christians are sad and depressed. They think it will continue like this till Christ returns. But God through Zechariah is encouraging us. Better days are round the corner.

1. The Man with the Measuring Line (vv1-2)

"I lifted up mine eyes again, and looked, and behold a man with a measuring line in his hand. Then said I, Whither goest thou? And he said unto me, To measure Jerusalem, to see what is the breadth thereof, and what is the length thereof."

Jerusalem at this time was in ruins. The Chaldeans from Babylon had broken down the walls, destroyed the palaces and burnt the temple. The inhabitants had been carried away captive. For seventy years the land had been desolate. Now a relatively small number of the exiles have returned. They set up an altar and began the worship of God again in Jerusalem. They started to build the temple, but became discouraged. They were few in number. They had nothing like the resources which Solomon had when he built the first temple. They were surrounded by enemies who tried to frighten them and stop the work. The economic situation was difficult.

They had to build homes for themselves and cultivate fields. It is easy to focus on the difficulties and despair takes over. Some thought they would never be able to complete the building of the temple. They thought Jerusalem was always going to remain a ruin. Surely God has forsaken them. He has justly been angry with them. Their sins have been awful and it looks as if God has cast them off forever. But here is a fascinating vision. God shows Zechariah that there is a future. Here is a surveyor, a builder, with a measuring line in His hand. Preparations are being made to rebuild. God Himself is involved. The city will be built again. We have here an encouraging vision for Zechariah, for the Jews at that time, but also for the true church of God today.

2. Jerusalem Crowded (vv3-4)

"And, behold, the angel that talked with me went forth, and another angel went out to meet him, And said unto him, Run, speak to this young man, saying, Jerusalem shall be inhabited as towns without walls for the multitude of men and cattle therein."

An angel was showing these visions to Zechariah. Another angel comes to meet this angel and has a wonderful message to declare: "Run, speak to this young man, saying, Jerusalem shall be inhabited as towns without walls for the multitude of men and cattle therein" (v4). At the time very few lived in Jerusalem. It had no walls and there was little security for the residents. Seventy-five years after this in the days of Nehemiah the walls of Jerusalem would eventually be rebuilt. Even at that later date special measures had to be used to conscript people to live in Jerusalem. Some were praised for volunteering to live there. There had to be a certain number of inhabitants to make it a viable city. But here it is predicted that walls will not be able to hold the multitudes who will come to stay in Jerusalem. Later Jerusalem did grow, but it was then a walled city. Similarly, in the time of Jesus, Jerusalem had a considerable population but these were enclosed within the city walls. When the Romans destroyed Jerusalem in 70AD they had to lay siege to the city for five months before they broke through the walls. When was this prophecy fulfilled? It is surely yet to be fulfilled. The church becomes the New Jerusalem. In the New Testament age it will grow and grow. On the day of Pentecost 3000 were added to the church. This number of members soon greatly increased. The Church has now grown till it is to be found as a minority in every country of the world. But the true church is still only a tiny minority of the world's population. Surely this passage speaks not of a handful here and there but of a great multitude. We think of our own congregations. How small they are! Here, though, there is reference to overflowing numbers. God's church will be as towns without walls for the multitude of men and cattle therein. We look in faith and optimism for a day when our churches will have standing room only and crowds will be standing outside trying to get in.

3. God Protects (v5)

"For I, saith the Lord, will be unto her a wall of fire round about, and will be the glory in the midst of her."

To people in ancient times a town without walls was very vulnerable. Enemies could easily attack under cover of darkness. But here is a promise. God says, "I…will be unto her a wall of fire round about, and will be the glory in the midst of her." When Nebuchadnezzar attacked Jerusalem the city had powerful walls but yet they could not keep him out. The siege weakened the defenders and bit by bit the battering rams broke the walls. But if Jerusalem had a wall of divine fire around her who could penetrate that? When the horses and chariots of Egypt were following the Israelites at the Red Sea, God was a barrier between them and the Israelites. He was a pillar of fire giving light to Israel and a cloud of darkness to the Egyptians. The king Ahaziah sent a captain of fifty with his fifty men to arrest the prophet Elijah who was sitting on a hill. He said to the prophet, "Thou man of God, the king hath said, Come down" (2 Kings 1:9). The Prophet replied, "If I be a man of God, then let fire come down from heaven, and consume thee and thy fifty" (v10). Then fire came down from heaven, and consumed him and his fifty. The king sent another captain with fifty men. This man demanded, "O man of God, thus hath the king said, Come down quickly" (v11). Again, the prophet replied, "If I be a man of God, let fire come down from heaven, and consume thee and thy fifty. And the fire of God came down from heaven, and consumed him and his fifty" (v12). God was a wall of fire protecting his prophet. No army could hurt him. When the king sent a further captain with his fifty men, "The third captain of fifty went up, and came and fell on his knees before Elijah, and besought him, and said unto him, O man of God, I pray thee, let my life, and the life of these fifty thy servants, be precious in thy sight. Behold, there came fire down from heaven, and burnt up the two captains of the former fifties with their fifties: therefore let my life now be precious in thy sight" (vv13-14). This captain knew full well that no matter how large his army was and how well equipped they were, they were helpless before the fire of God.

The new Jerusalem is the church of God. The church has many enemies today. Some are politically powerful and ruthless. Others are clever and sophisticated. But the church is safe because God is a wall of fire around her. Jesus said, "Upon this rock I will build my church; and the gates of hell shall not prevail against it" (Matthew 16:18). In the city gates the leaders gathered and made their plans. All the cunning of hell is organised against God's church. But Christ will build His church and nothing can hinder or destroy it. Nothing can hold back the advance of the church of Christ because He is building His church.

We are also told here that God, "will be the glory in the midst of her" (v5). That was wonderfully true of Israel as she travelled from Egypt to the Promised Land. God was present among her as the Shekinah glory. The pillar of cloud by day and the pillar of fire by night led Israel and when they encamped the pillar of God's presence rested on the Tabernacle. When the temple was built the presence of God filled the Holy of Holies, between the cherubim upon the mercy-seat.

In Ezekiel's prophecy we are told of the dramatic departure of the glory of God's presence. First, we are told that "The glory of the God of Israel was gone up from the cherub, whereupon he was, to the threshold of the house" (Ezekiel 9:3). Then in the following chapter we read: "Then the glory of the Lord departed from off the threshold of the house, and stood over the cherubims. And the cherubims lifted up their wings, and mounted up from the earth in my sight: when they went out, the wheels also were beside them, and every one stood at the door of the east gate of the Lord's house; and the glory of the God of Israel was over them above" (Ezekiel 10:18-19). Finally in the following chapter it is stated, "Then did the cherubims lift up their wings, and the wheels beside them; and the glory of the God of Israel was over them above. And the glory of the Lord went up from the midst of the city, and stood upon the mountain which is on the east side of the city" (Ezekiel 11:22-23). The glory of the Lord had departed from Jerusalem.

But now we read that God will be the glory in the midst of her. There is no reference of the glory of the Lord coming down upon the second temple. It was stated however through the prophet Haggai, "The glory of this latter house shall be greater than of the former, saith the Lord of hosts: and in this place will I give peace, saith the Lord of hosts" (Haggai 2:9). This was because the Messiah, who is God Himself, would condescend to enter it and teach in it. That second temple was destroyed by the Jews when they crucified Christ, but in three days he raised up the new, eternal temple. Jesus said, "Destroy this temple, and in three days I will raise it up. Then said the Jews, Forty and six years was this temple in building, and wilt thou rear it up in three days? But he spake of the temple of his body" (John 2:19-21). This new temple is His church. It is composed of living stones, believers, and Christ Himself is the chief cornerstone. This temple is indwelt by the Holy Spirit, and so has the glory of God in the midst.

4. Separate yourselves from the Heathen (vv6-7)

"Ho, ho, come forth, and flee from the land of the north, saith the Lord: for I have spread you abroad as the four winds of the heaven, saith the Lord. Deliver thyself, O Zion, that dwellest with the daughter of Babylon."

The land of the north was Assyria first, then Babylon and eventually Persia. These empires were to the east but they always invaded from the north. God had scattered Israel abroad. In His wrath against His people because of their idolatry, they were carried away captive and God had scattered them among the heathen. But now His purpose is to gather them again to the land of Israel. Assyria and Babylon had been destroyed. The Jews are to separate themselves from the nations. Sadly, too many Jews were comfortable in Mesopotamia. They had nice houses and good jobs and businesses. But God's wrath is against the heathen nations and He is going to destroy them. He warns His people, "Deliver thyself, O Zion, that dwellest with the daughter of Babylon." Do not perish with the heathen.

The same message comes to us today. Paul warns the Corinthian believers: "Be ye not unequally yoked together with unbelievers: for what fellowship hath righteousness with unrighteousness? and what communion hath light with darkness? And what concord hath Christ with Belial? or what part hath he that believeth with an infidel? And what agreement hath the temple of God with idols? For ye are the temple of the living God; as God hath said, I will dwell in them, and walk in them; and I will be their God, and they shall be my people. Wherefore come out from among them, and be ye separate, saith the Lord, and touch not the unclean thing; and I will receive you. And will be a Father unto you, and ye shall be my sons and daughters, saith the Lord Almighty" (2 Corinthians 6:14-18). Marrying the unconverted or entering into a close business relationship with such is condemned. It will almost always lead to compromise. Christians and unbelievers are opposites. Christians love God but non-christians hate God. If we love and follow God, we will be hated by those who love Satan and his ways.

Similar teaching is to be found in the Book of Revelation with reference to the apostate church: "Come out of her, my people, that ye be not partakers of her sins, and that ye receive not of her plagues. For her sins have reached unto heaven, and God hath remembered her iniquities. Reward her even as she rewarded you, and double unto her double according to her works: in the cup which she hath filled fill to her double"

(Revelation 18:4-6). God's true people are not to be members of the church of the Antichrist, or of bodies that teach heresy and practise immorality.

The Jews are to return to Jerusalem. God's people are to be holy people not unequally yoked with the wicked. True Christians are to separate themselves from the sacramentalism and idolatry of the Roman Catholic and the Eastern Orthodox Churches, and the liberal unbelief of so many mainline Protestant churches.

5. God will be glorified in destroying His enemies (vv8-9)

"For thus saith the Lord of hosts; After the glory hath he sent me unto the nations which spoiled you: for he that toucheth you toucheth the apple of his eye. For, behold, I will shake mine hand upon them, and they shall be a spoil to their servants: and ye shall know that the Lord of hosts hath sent me."

"After the glory hath he sent me unto the nations which spoiled you." God will at the last get the glory. His enemies will ultimately all be destroyed. They laugh at God's people and mock them but the Lord is grieved for His people and concerned for His own great name. His enemies will be trampled underfoot. The seed of the woman shall bruise the serpent's head. Christ will crush Satan and all his followers. Those who spoiled the church will be spoiled. The enemies of the church touch the apple of God's eye. How special you are to God, you who are a child of His! He loves you with an infinite, eternal and unchangeable love. Isaiah wrote: "I will mention the loving-kindnesses of the Lord, and the praises of the Lord, according to all that the Lord hath bestowed on us, and the great goodness toward the house of Israel, which he hath bestowed on them according to his mercies, and according to the multitude of his loving-kindnesses" (Isaiah 63:7). He is bound in covenant love to His people, therefore, "In all their affliction he was afflicted, and the angel of his presence saved them: in his love and in his pity he redeemed them; and he bare them, and carried them all the days of old" (Isaiah 63:9). Our great King states, "I will tread them in mine anger, and trample them in my fury; and their blood shall be sprinkled upon my garments, and I will stain all my raiment. For the day of vengeance is in mine heart, and the year of my redeemed is come" (Isaiah 63:3-4).

The Angel of the Lord, who is speaking here, is obviously the Second Person of the Trinity, the Lord Himself, for He adds, "Behold, I will shake mine hand upon them, and they shall be a spoil to their servants: and ye shall know that the Lord of hosts hath sent me" (v9). That shaking of the hand destroys the leaders of their enemies so that they become a spoil to their own servants. The end result will be that all will acknowledge that Jesus Christ is Lord to the glory of God the Father (Philippians 2:11).

6. Sing in Triumph (v10)

"Sing and rejoice, O daughter of Zion: for, lo, I come, and I will dwell in the midst of thee, saith the Lord."

Too often God's people are depressed and downcast. The Jews here are commanded to sing for joy. We often sigh and groan. No! Remember what Paul said, "Rejoice in the Lord always: and again I say, Rejoice" (Philippians 4:4). "We are more than conquerors through him that loved us" (Romans 8:37). "What shall we then say to these things? If God be for us, who can be against us?" (Romans 8:31). Let us sing for joy. No longer will God be a stranger to us. He will not be our enemy. He promises to come and dwell in our midst. We pray, "Oh that thou wouldest rend the heavens, that thou wouldest come down" (Isaiah 64:1), but now He assures us He will come and He will dwell with us. He has further assured us, "I will never leave thee, nor forsake thee. So that we may boldly say, The Lord is my helper, and I will not fear what man shall do unto me" (Hebrews 13:5-6). Let us from our hearts sing His praises and rejoice in Him.

7. Many nations will be united to Israel (v11)

And many nations shall be joined to the Lord in that day, and shall be my people: and I will dwell in the midst of thee, and thou shalt know that the Lord of hosts hath sent me unto thee.

This prophecy is obviously not limited to Israel and Judah. Many nations are going to come and be united with them. This happened in the New Testament times. Christ commanded that the gospel was to be preached to all nations. Following Pentecost, the church spread to the Gentile world. Down through the centuries all nations have been touched, but so far only a remnant from them. Surely there is a promise here that not just a few from these nations but the nations themselves considered as a whole will come. We look forward to great multitudes being gathered into the church of God. They shall belong to God just as Israel did. God Himself will dwell in these nations and He will be their God. All shall know that this prophecy is the truth sent by the Lord of hosts through His prophet.

8. God's People will be His Portion (v12)

"And the Lord shall inherit Judah his portion in the holy land, and shall choose Jerusalem again."

God has chosen Judah and Jerusalem. It has seemed at times that he is not interested in them and has forgotten them, but that is not the case. They are His delight and have a great future before them. This is true of the literal Judah and Jerusalem for as Paul states, "The gifts and calling of God are without repentance" (Rom.11:29). We are looking for the natural branch to be grafted again into the olive tree. But these words are true of all God's people, Jew or Gentile. They are his portion and delight. We receive God as our inheritance and God takes us as His inheritance.

9. You enemies, be silent! (v13)

"Be silent, O all flesh, before the Lord: for he is raised up out of his holy habitation."

For a long time it seemed that God was asleep. His people were being trampled upon by their enemies. He allowed their enemies to gain the victory over them because of their backsliding. But now He arises to deal with their enemies. As the Psalmist puts it: "Then the Lord awaked as one out of sleep, and like a mighty man that shouteth by reason of wine. And he smote his enemies in the hinder parts: he put them to a perpetual reproach" (Psalms 78:65-66). Though God seems to be sleeping He is soon going to awake. Let us pray as Isaiah did: "Awake, awake, put on strength, O arm of the Lord; awake, as in the ancient days, in the generations of old. Art thou not it that hath cut Rahab, and wounded the dragon? Art thou not it which hath dried the sea, the waters of the great deep; that hath made the depths of the sea a way for the ransomed to pass over?" (Isaiah 51:9-10). Let the enemies of the church be silent and frightened. God has stirred Himself up. He will severely punish those whom He used to chastise His people. His church has a great future.

CHAPTER 5

FOURTH VISION: JOSHUA THE HIGH PRIEST

(Zechariah 3)

In Zechariah Chapter 3, we have the fourth vision given to the prophet. It is quite different from the previous three but at the same time it is also very encouraging. We all have one great problem and that is our sin. As a result of the sin of Adam we are all born sinners. Sin is natural for us. It is easy for us to break God's law. Sadly, we sin constantly in thought, word and deed. The Psalmist says concerning himself, and it is true of us all, "Behold, I was shapen in iniquity; and in sin did my mother conceive me" (Psalm 51:5). In this, he is not referring to the act of procreation. There is nothing sinful in that for it is written, "Marriage is honourable in all, and the bed undefiled" (Hebrews 13:4). Rather, it is a statement regarding our moral condition from the very beginning of our existence. We sinned in Adam and fell with him in his first transgression. Even before our conception or actual existence, we were sinners because we were included in the covenant made with Adam. In the original covenant that God made with all mankind Adam acted as the representative of all those who would descend from him by ordinary generation. As a result of Adam's first sin the nature of every man and woman is fallen and depraved. Thus Paul asserts concerning himself and the Ephesian Christians, "And you hath he quickened, who were dead in trespasses and sins; Wherein in time past ye walked according to the course of this world, according to the prince of the power of the air, the spirit that now worketh in the children of disobedience: Among whom also we all had our conversation in times past in the lusts of our flesh, fulfilling the desires of the flesh and of the mind; and were by nature the children of wrath, even as others" (Ephesians 2:1-

3). Our condition by birth is one on total depravity and total inability. We begin life dead to God and wallowing in our sin.

Salvation is the work of God from beginning to end. To Him must go all the glory. God planned it, sent His Son to earn it for us on the cross and now sends His Spirit into our hearts to apply it to us. Thus Paul, having spoken of our helpless condition of being dead in our sins, proceeds to describe God's intervention for us: "But God, who is rich in mercy, for his great love wherewith he loved us, even when we were dead in sins, hath quickened us together with Christ, (by grace ye are saved) and hath raised us up together, and made us sit together in heavenly places in Christ Jesus: that in the ages to come he might shew the exceeding riches of his grace in his kindness toward us through Christ Jesus. For by grace are ye saved through faith; and that not of yourselves: it is the gift of God: not of works, lest any man should boast" (Ephesians 2:4-9). Praise be to God for our salvation! It is all His work from beginning to end and all glory must be given to Him.

However, even after our conversion, sadly, we still sin and sin. Yes, there has been a huge change. We are no longer dead in sin. Sin bothers us. We hate it. It does not rule over us. Yet we must constantly battle against it. Again, Paul described the struggles of himself and other Christians: "When I would do good, evil is present with me. For I delight in the law of God after the inward man: But I see another law in my members, warring against the law of my mind, and bringing me into captivity to the law of sin which is in my members. O wretched man that I am! who shall deliver me from the body of this death?" (Romans 7:21-24). The Christian's life is one of constant warfare against the world, the flesh and the devil.

The vision here given to the prophet is a very encouraging one. Yes we are sinners. We deserve hell. But God loves us and has made provision for us. Satan says "You are a disgrace. Don't try to pray. God hates you because of your sin. Stay out of His presence. There is no hope for you. You might as well go on sinning." But Satan, the cunning serpent, is a liar when he says God hates us and that there is no point in us praying to God. We must not let sin be a barrier to us drawing near to the Lord. There are many encouragements given to us to repent, confess our sin and draw near again to God. "God commendeth his love toward us, in that, while we were yet sinners, Christ died for us. Much more then, being now justified by his blood, we shall be saved from wrath through him" (Romans 5:8-9). John assures us, "If any man sin, we have an advocate with the Father, Jesus Christ the righteous" (1 John 2:1). Further, he writes, "The blood of Jesus Christ his Son cleanseth us from all sin… If we confess our sins, he is faithful and just to forgive us our sins, and to cleanse us from all unrighteousness" (1 John 1:7, 9). The vision before us illustrates these truths in a very graphic way.

1. Joshua the High Priest (v1)

"And he shewed me Joshua the high priest standing before the angel of the Lord, and Satan standing at his right hand to resist him."

The high priest was the one who in Old Testament times led the worship of God's people. Satan is the great enemy of God and therefore of God's people. He stands at the priest's right hand to resist him, mock him and accuse him. Because Satan cannot attack God directly, he does all he can to trouble and hurt the people of God. He knows that God loves His people so if he can get God's people to sin or if he can stop God's people from worshipping God and serving God as they should, he thinks he hurts God. But God cannot be hurt. He is the blessed and happy One. He sees the end from the beginning. Satan will be punished for ever and God will be glorified in the salvation of His people despite all Satan's cunning. Satan will be crushed. His doom is approaching rapidly.

2. Satan Rebuked (v2)

"And the Lord said unto Satan, The Lord rebuke thee, O Satan; even the Lord that hath chosen Jerusalem rebuke thee: is not this a brand plucked out of the fire?"

God has a special relationship with His people. He has chosen them from eternity and not because of anything good in them. He has loved them with an eternal love. His love is infinite and it is like Himself, unchangeable. We can be confident in this, "That he which hath begun a good work in you will perform it until the day of Jesus Christ" (Philippians 1:6).

Satan points to Joshua's sins and to our sins. Joshua is not only carrying his own personal sin and guilt but also, as the high priest, he carries the sin of the people. Satan says, "You deserve to be punished in hell forever" and he is right. But we can point to Calvary and say to Satan that Christ is our substitute and has stood in our place, carried all our sins and borne all the punishment which we deserved. When Satan accuses us of the worst of sins we can say, "There is therefore now no condemnation to them which are in Christ Jesus" (Romans 8:1) and also, "being justified by faith, we have peace with God through our Lord Jesus Christ" (Romans 5:1). We can further challenge him with the words, "Who shall lay any thing to the charge of God's elect? It is God that justifieth. Who is he that condemneth? It is Christ that died, yea rather, that is risen again, who is even at the right hand of God, who also maketh intercession for us" (Romans 8:33-34).

Here God says to Satan, "The Lord rebuke thee, O Satan." Jerusalem was a most rebellious city, but yet it was the city God chose out of all the cities of the earth to place His name there. Joshua and Jerusalem stand together. The high priest stands for the city and nation. A great statement is made, "Is not this a brand plucked out of the fire?" That was true of Joshua, and it was true of Jerusalem and it is true of the church today. Joshua was spared. He was to be destroyed by a righteous and holy God, but another took his place. Similarly, Jerusalem was destroyed by the Chaldeans but it is now emerging from the ashes like a brand plucked from the fire. We look at the church today. It is so weak. The world has infiltrated and invaded it and taken it over. The church is so dead that it appears to be doomed. But God picks the brand from the fire. God will have His church. The gates of hell will not prevail against it. To man the situation seems hopeless but it is never so to God. When all hope is lost He steps in and shows that He cares deeply and He has a great plan for His people. We must never despair.

3. Joshua's filthy Garments (v3)

"Now Joshua was clothed with filthy garments, and stood before the angel."

The Angel here is the Angel of the Covenant. It is God, the second person of the Trinity, and He is the One who appears in all the theophanies in the Old Testament. The High Priest's clothes are described as filthy. The word used here is very strong. His clothes are as it were covered with dung. What priest would dare appear before God at the altar with such filthy clothes? Satan stands at his right hand to accuse him. Surely Satan is right? Joshua is a disgrace. But was there ever a high priest who could draw near in his own righteousness? Every high priest from Aaron onwards was a sinner and, in that sense, totally unfit for approaching God. The only One who was "holy, harmless undefiled, separate from sinners" (Hebrews 7:26) was the Lord Jesus Christ, a priest after the order of Melchizedek, the final and greatest High Priest, the Priest whom we need, of whom all others were but types and pictures.

4. Take off the Filthy Garments (v4)

"And he answered and spake unto those that stood before him, saying, Take away the filthy garments from him. And unto him he said, Behold, I have caused thine iniquity to pass from thee, and I will clothe thee with change of raiment."

Here we have a wonderful truth set before us. The filthy garments are taken off Joshua. They are placed instead upon our Lord Jesus. He takes our rags and gives to us Christ's pure white robe of His righteousness. We are taught here the great Reformation doctrine of justification by faith alone. In every other religion, priests and men stand before God in their self-righteousness. No provision is made for sinners. Priests must try very hard to impress God with their clean garments. Sadly, however, the very best of men are sinners. We all sin in thought, word and deed constantly. In the eyes of an infinitely holy and just God we are all clothed in defiled and stinking garments. Jesus taught us, when we have achieved our very best, and tried our hardest, "When ye shall have done all those things which are commanded you, say, We are unprofitable servants: we have done that which was our duty to do" (Luke 17:10). The moment we put our faith in Jesus we are perfectly justified and accepted as righteous in the eyes of our holy God, and the Lord Jesus says to us as He said to the notorious sinner woman: "Thy sins are forgiven…Thy faith hath saved thee, go in peace" (Luke 7:48, 50).

The word used here in the Hebrew for "change of raiment" has the idea of festive garments and joyous, celebratory clothes. How wonderful! One moment Joshua is clothed with dirty garments and is standing there in shame with Satan laughing at him and the next moment he is covered in beautiful clean celebratory robes. Now it is Satan's turn to be ashamed. The accuser of the brethren has nothing to say. In the book of Revelation we find the words, "And I heard a loud voice saying in heaven, Now is come salvation, and strength, and the kingdom of our God, and the power of his Christ: for the "accuser of the brethren" is cast down, which accused them before our God day and night" (Revelation 12:10). Satan is called the "accuser of the brethren," but he is cast down.

5. Clothe him Afresh (v5)

"And I said, Let them set a fair mitre upon his head. So they set a fair mitre upon his head, and clothed him with garments. And the angel of the Lord stood by."

The Aaronic high priest had a mitre, or a kind of turban with a solid gold plate attached to the front of it which had the words engraved on it, "Holiness to the Lord" (Exodus 28:36). Where does this holiness come from? Again, it comes from Christ. He imparts holiness to us and by His Spirit sanctifies us. Paul wrote to the Corinthians, "But of him are ye in Christ Jesus, who of God is made unto us wisdom, and righteousness, and sanctification, and redemption: that, according as it is written, He that glorieth, let him glory in the Lord" (1 Corinthians 1:30-31). Christ earned it all for His people. Christ is our sanctification and Paul exhorts us, "But put ye on the Lord Jesus Christ, and make not provision for the flesh, to fulfil the lusts thereof" (Romans 13:14). Helped by the Spirit we are to put off our sins and clothe ourselves with Christ. No one can get into heaven without the wedding garment (Matthew 22:11-13).

6. The Lord's Encouragement (vv6-7)

"And the angel of the Lord protested unto Joshua, saying, Thus saith the Lord of hosts; If thou wilt walk in my ways, and if thou wilt keep my charge, then thou shalt also judge my house, and shalt also keep my courts, and I will give thee places to walk among these that stand by."

These are solemn words. Joshua has been justified but he now has the duty to live a holy life. Yes, we as God's people have been justified, and all our sins past, present, and future have been pardoned, but now we must walk in His ways. The priest and the people have a great obligation laid upon them. We must not think because our sins are forgiven that we can continue in sin. To do that would demonstrate that we have never been born again. It would show that our nature had not been changed and that we are still unconverted. It would demonstrate that we have never really believed in Jesus with saving faith. In point of fact, faith in Christ is impossible until we are regenerated. Paul wrote to the Romans: "What shall we say then? Shall we continue in sin, that grace may abound? God forbid. How shall we, that are dead to sin, live any longer therein?" (Romans 6:1-2). A person who is converted has experienced a huge change. Someone who is born again hates sin. Paul exhorted the Philippians: "Wherefore, my beloved, as ye have always obeyed, not as in my presence only, but now much more in my absence, work out your own salvation with fear and trembling. For it is God which worketh in you both to will and to do of his good pleasure" (Philippians 2:12-13). We must work at saving ourselves but, at the same time we must remember that it is God who is working in us, giving us the desire and the ability. The promise is made to Joshua the son of Josedech that if he will obey the Lord he will judge God's house and keep His courts and lead His people and be given his place among the courtiers of heaven.

7. The Branch (v8)

"Hear now, O Joshua the high priest, thou, and thy fellows that sit before thee: for they are men wondered at: for, behold, I will bring forth my servant the Branch."

Interestingly, there were no seats in the temple. The priests were constantly ministering and offering sacrifices which could never take away sin (Hebrews 10:1-2). Their work was never finished. But the priests here gathered before Joshua have completed their work and therefore are seated. The one great sacrifice has made atonement for sin for ever. It is finished. They are seated. "Men wondered at…", that is, because they are types and symbols of Jesus Christ the great High Priest who having made atonement for our sins sat down at the right hand of God.

"For, behold, I will bring forth my servant the Branch." What we have here is a very clear prophecy of the coming Messiah. He is called "my servant." This is in line with the servant songs of Isaiah. The most famous begins, "Behold, my servant shall deal prudently, he shall be exalted and extolled, and be very high" (Isaiah 52:13). Interestingly you also get a picture of the Branch or Shoot: "For he shall grow up before him as a tender plant, and as a root out of a dry ground: he hath no form nor comeliness; and when we shall see him, there is no beauty that we should desire him" (Isaiah 53:2). He is the rejected One, despised, wounded, bruised, chastised and "he was cut off out of the land of the living: for the transgression of my people was he stricken" (v8). "Yet it pleased the Lord to bruise him; he hath put him to grief: when thou shalt make his soul an offering for sin, he shall see his seed, he shall prolong his days, and the pleasure of the Lord shall prosper in his hand" (v10). The Lord was pleased with his Servant because he carried out His will for the salvation of the elect, "he bare the sin of many, and made intercession for the transgressors" (v12).

The Branch here is the Son of David who is also David's Lord: "The Lord said unto my Lord, Sit thou at my right hand, until I make thine enemies thy footstool. The Lord shall send the rod of thy strength out of Zion: rule thou in the midst of thine enemies" (Psalm 110:1-2). According to his humanity he is a child of David but he is also the Son of God. He needed to be divine, as well as human, to carry out this great work. As He himself said, "I am the root and the offspring of David, and the bright and morning star" (Revelation 22:16). He is the Root of David as God, and He is the Shoot or Branch of David as a man and David's son. He is the fruitful Branch who has many children. His travailing will not be in vain, "He shall see of the travail of his soul, and shall be satisfied: by his knowledge shall my righteous servant justify many; for he shall bear their iniquities" (Isaiah 53:11).

8. The Stone (v9)

"For behold the stone that I have laid before Joshua; upon one stone shall be seven eyes: behold, I will engrave the graving thereof, saith the Lord of hosts, and I will remove the iniquity of that land in one day."

The picture is changed from the Branch to a Stone. These men were building the temple. Here is the most critical stone of all, "The stone which the builders refused is become the head stone of the corner" (Psalm 118:22). The Stone is another representation of the one who is the Branch. The Lord Jesus was rejected in His day by the Pharisees and Sadducees, but He is become the chief cornerstone. He is the great stone which holds the building together. The true and lasting temple is based on Him. The stone has seven eyes and these are the seven spirits of God or the Holy Spirit in the fullness of His power who equipped Christ for His work. The stone is engraved, like the plate on the mitre with "Holiness to the Lord." He removes the iniquity of Israel in one day and the end result is heaven. We have here, then, a wonderful prophecy of Christ and His work.

9. Peace (v10)

"In that day, saith the Lord of hosts, shall ye call every man his neighbour under the vine and under the fig tree."

The Lord here is disclosing the future to the prophet and to Israel. There are wonderful days coming. The One who is the Branch and the Stone shall come. There shall be an age of great peace and prosperity. We have here the idyllic picture of every man calling his neighbour to sit and talk with him under his vine and under his fig tree. It surely speaks of glorious times ahead for the church of God, but especially of the promised land of heaven above.

CHAPTER 6

FIFTH VISION: THE GOLDEN LAMPSTAND

(Zechariah 4)

Of all Zechariah's visions this is my favourite one. In these days in Scotland and indeed in the whole Western World, it is easy to become discouraged. Church attendances are small. Most of the population show no interest in God. We have the glorious gospel of our Lord Jesus Christ, telling how God became man to save us, how He died on the cross in our room and stead, bearing our sins and the punishment due to us, how He rose again on the third day having completed the work of atonement, and how He now calls all men and women to repent and believe and so to be saved, be adopted into God's family, and have a place with Him in heaven when we die. But most people show no interest. Many no longer believe in God. The theory of evolution is accepted as explaining how everything came into existence following a "big bang." People have comfortable lives with no great financial needs. They are doped by entertainment and have little time or clarity of head to think seriously. If there is a God, the churches generally portray Him as a God of love who is no threat to anyone. There is little preaching of hell so there is no fear of God's wrath. The churches' message, for example on sexual behaviour, is confused and woolly therefore ignored. Man, in his self-righteousness, thinks of himself as relatively good so that even if there is a hell, he thinks, God surely won't send him there. What need there is for an outpouring of the Holy Spirit to convict and "reprove the world of sin, and of righteousness, and of judgment" (John 16:8)! We need God to intervene and to shake men and women out of their apathy. We cry with Isaiah of old, "Oh that thou wouldest rend the heavens, that thou wouldest come down" (Isaiah 64:1).

This chapter, though, encourages us. It tells us that God will build His church. We are to look up to heaven and rejoice in the sovereign Lord who is working out His purposes for the salvation of His people.

1. The Church Pictured (vv1-3)

"And the angel that talked with me came again, and waked me, as a man that is wakened out of his sleep. And said unto me, What seest thou? And I said, I have looked, and behold a candlestick all of gold, with a bowl upon the top of it, and his seven lamps thereon, and seven pipes to the seven lamps, which are upon the top thereof: And two olive trees by it, one upon the right side of the bowl, and the other upon the left side thereof."

The angel returns to Zechariah to show him more visions. Here, it seems to him, that he is wakened out of this sleep and he is asked what he sees. First, he sees a candlestick or rather a lampstand made of gold. It would remind him of the lampstand, the menorah, in the tabernacle and in the temple. It was a type of Christ who is the light of the world but also it symbolises God's people, the Israelites in the Old Testament and the church today. Christ shines through them. He says "I am the light of the world" (John 8:12). But He also says to his followers, "Ye are the light of the world" (Matthew 5:14). You are not the source of light but rather you are to transmit My light. Be a candlestick to the world: "Neither do men light a candle, and put it under a bushel, but on a candlestick; and it giveth light unto all that are in the house. Let your light so shine before men, that they may see your good works, and glorify your Father which is in heaven" (Matthew 5:15-16). There is no light in us of ourselves but we are to reflect the light of Christ to mankind. The church is the body of Christ and the church existed in the Old Testament too. The Jews were the church in Zechariah's day.

Our understanding of this is clarified in the Book of Revelation. There we come across the lampstands again when the Apostle John is given a vision of Christ, "And I turned to see the voice that spake with me. And being turned, I saw seven golden candlesticks; And in the midst of the seven candlesticks one like unto the Son of man" (Revelation 1:12-13).

This vision is then explained, "The mystery of the seven stars which thou sawest in my right hand, and the seven golden candlesticks. The seven stars are the angels of the seven churches: and the seven candlesticks which thou sawest are the seven churches" (Revelation 1:20). So here we are specifically told that the candlesticks represent the seven churches of Asia.

The church of God is composed of the elect who have come to faith in Christ. In Old Testament times they looked forward in faith to the One who was to come and be the Lamb of God taking away the sin of the world. In the New Testament age we look back in faith to Calvary and the finished work of Christ on the Cross. This is, "the church of God, which he hath purchased with his own blood" (Acts 20:28). Patriarchs like Abel, Enoch and Noah belonged to it. It was first organised separately in the days of Abraham when he was told to circumcise his children and place upon them the token of the covenant (Genesis 17). The sign of circumcision is later described as a "seal of the righteousness of the faith" (Romans 4:11). It was a sign and seal of the covenant of grace and marked out the church of the Old Testament just as baptism marks the church of the New Testament.

The world lies in the darkness of ignorance and sin. It is dominated by the Prince of Darkness, the Devil. The church gives light. It transmits the light of Christ who is "the true Light, which lighteth every man that cometh into the world" (John 1:9). Our light is not from ourselves. By nature we have no light in us. It is only as Christ by His Spirit comes to reside in our hearts that we can truly shine forth. God said, "Ye are my witnesses, saith the Lord, and my servant whom I have chosen: that ye may know and believe me, and understand that I am he: before me there was no God formed, neither shall there be after me. I, even I, am the Lord; and beside me there is no saviour" (Isaiah 43:10-11).

The lampstand is all of gold. This speaks of its value. In the eyes of the world the church is despised but God sees it as really precious: "They shall be mine, saith the Lord of hosts, in that day when I make up my jewels; and I will spare them, as a man spareth his own son that serveth him" (Malachi 3:17). Gold has a durability about it. Iron will rust and silver tarnish, but gold continues to shine. There is a certain purity about gold and so God's church, washed in the blood, is without spot or blemish. Further, it has seven lamps. Seven is the number of the church and the number of perfection. There are two olive trees by the lampstand, one on the right side and the other on the left. These produce a constant supply of oil for the lamps so that they keep shining.

2. The Power of the Church (vv4-6)

"So I answered and spake to the angel that talked with me, saying, What are these, my lord? Then the angel that talked with me answered and said unto me, Knowest thou not what these be? And I said, No, my lord. Then he answered and spake unto me, saying, This is the word of the Lord unto Zerubbabel, saying, Not by might, nor by power, but by my spirit, saith the Lord of hosts."

What a contrast there was between the days of Zechariah and that of David and Solomon. When the first temple was built the wealth that David and Solomon had gathered was immense. Solomon had a huge labour force at his disposal and many highly-skilled and gifted craftsmen. The temple in earthly terms was truly magnificent. Zerubbabel and Joshua could not hope to build anything like it in glory. There was this huge project before them and it was easy to be paralysed by the immensity of the challenge. When we struggle to build God's church today, we are conscious that we do not have great Reformers such as Martin Luther, John Calvin and John Knox. We do not have deep theologians like John Owen, Jonathan Edwards, and Benjamin Warfield. We do not have mighty preachers and evangelists like George Whitefield and C. H. Spurgeon. We are few in number, and none of us is particularly gifted. But we must remember what is said here: "Not by might, nor by power, but by my spirit, saith the Lord of hosts." It is not human gifts which make the difference, but the divine blessing. "Cease ye from man, whose breath is in his nostrils: for wherein is he to be accounted of?" (Isaiah 2:22). Do not look to man to provide the answers. Man at best is feeble. Isaiah records that "The voice said, Cry. And he said, What shall I cry? All flesh is grass, and all the goodliness thereof is as the flower of the field: The grass withereth, the flower fadeth:

because the spirit of the Lord bloweth upon it: surely the people is grass. The grass withereth, the flower fadeth: but the word of our God shall stand for ever" (Isaiah 40:6-8). Do not trust in man. Look up! Put your faith in God. Seek the help of His Spirit. Human might and power will fail but when the Spirit of God begins a work He will finish it: "Being confident of this very thing, that he which hath begun a good work in you will perform it until the day of Jesus Christ" (Philippians 1:6). Here, then, there is tremendous encouragement for us in our weakness. It does not depend on us but on God. We look to God to revive His church. God promises miracles and the impossible becomes possible: "Who hath heard such a thing? who hath seen such things? Shall the earth be made to bring forth in one day? or shall a nation be born at once? for as soon as Zion travailed, she brought forth her children" (Isaiah 66:8). Yes, God assures us, a nation can be born again in a day. Let us labour in prayer for this.

3. Obstacles Overcome (v7)

"Who art thou, O great mountain? before Zerubbabel thou shalt become a plain: and he shall bring forth the headstone thereof with shoutings, crying, Grace, grace unto it."

It was hard for the returning exiles to build the temple. Mountains of rubbish had to be cleared away before the work could begin. New stones and timber had to be gathered and prepared. The Samaritans opposed the work and tried to stop it. For a while they succeeded. Some pessimists among the Jews felt sure that the enterprise would be a complete failure. They discouraged the workers. It is the same today. There are many enemies: the media, politicians, philosophers, leaders in education, social workers, 'woke' campaigners and the courts. Secularists and humanists are actively promoting their agenda. False religions and cults of every sort abound. There are mountains blocking our way. It seems that there is no way the church can be built up. But look at the promise here: "Who art thou, O great mountain? before Zerubbabel thou shalt become a plain." The mountains in the way are removed by God. Jesus said: "Have faith in

63

God. For verily I say unto you, That whosoever shall say unto this mountain, Be thou removed, and be thou cast into the sea; and shall not doubt in his heart, but shall believe that those things which he saith shall come to pass; he shall have whatsoever he saith" (Mark 11:22-23). If we have faith even as small as a mustard seed we can overcome every obstacle. We can move mountains of problems into the sea.

God is here assuring Zerubbabel that the work of building the temple will be successful. Unbelieving people say it will never be completed but Zerubbabel shall "bring forth the headstone thereof with shoutings, crying, Grace, grace unto it." The copestone or final stone will be placed. When that is done it will not be a matter of, "See the great work which I have done! Amn't I great!" But rather: "Grace, grace unto it." To God be all the glory! Nothing would have been achieved without Him. Praise be to God! It is like that in building God's church. All the glory must go to God. Nothing of lasting value is achieved without Him.

4. Assured Success (v8-9)

"Moreover the word of the Lord came unto me, saying, The hands of Zerubbabel have laid the foundation of this house; his hands shall also finish it; and thou shalt know that the Lord of hosts hath sent me unto you."

The hands of Zerubbabel, the governor, laid the foundation of the second temple and God assures both him and the people that his hands shall place the last stone in position. This is the word of the Lord and He never tells lies. His word will never fail and His promises are sure. When the Jews shall see the temple completed, they will have to confess that a prophet of the Lord has been among them. What tremendous encouragement this was to the struggling builders. We too have the words of an even greater Prophet, the Lord Jesus: "I will build my church; and the gates of hell shall not prevail against it" (Matthew 16:18). One day the New Testament temple will be complete. John tells us of the revelation he received of the church of God in her final perfect state. The angel who showed it to him said, "Come hither, I will shew thee the bride, the Lamb's wife. And he carried me away in the spirit to a great and high mountain, and shewed me that great city, the holy Jerusalem, descending out of heaven from God, Having the glory of God: and her light was like unto a stone most precious, even like a jasper stone, clear as crystal; And had a wall great and high, and had twelve gates, and at the gates twelve angels, and names written thereon, which are the names of the twelve tribes of the children of Israel: On the east three gates; on the north three gates; on the south three gates; and on the west three gates. And the wall of the city had twelve foundations, and in them the names of the twelve apostles of the Lamb" (Revelation 21:9-14). This is the church of God, the spiritual temple. John says that he saw no temple in it. That is because it is all temple. Success in building God's church is assured.

5. Sinful Pessimism (v10)

"For who hath despised the day of small things? for they shall rejoice, and shall see the plummet in the hand of Zerubbabel with those seven; they are the eyes of the Lord, which run to and fro through the whole earth."

Zechariah's day was a day of small things in that the Jews were weak and poor. Because they were few in number and not gifted, some pessimists said that nothing would be achieved. They were wasting their time trying to build a temple. Sometimes you and I feel that we are failures and are overwhelmed by the difficulties of building God's church. Even the Messiah is prophesied as saying words which many a minister has used, "I have laboured in vain, I have spent my strength for nought, and in vain" (Isaiah 49:4). But our Lord goes on to say, "Yet surely my judgment is with the Lord, and my work with my God." Then God assures Him: "And now, saith the Lord that formed me from the womb to be his servant, to bring Jacob again to him, Though Israel be not gathered, yet shall I be glorious in the eyes of the Lord, and my God shall be my strength. And he said, It is a light thing that thou shouldest be my servant to raise up the tribes of Jacob, and to restore the preserved of Israel: I will also give thee for a light to the Gentiles, that thou mayest be my salvation unto the end of the earth"

(Isaiah 49:5-6). The Messiah would restore the tribes of Jacob and even gather the Gentiles into the church. Later Isaiah declares, "He shall see of the travail of his soul, and shall be satisfied: by his knowledge shall my righteous servant justify many; for he shall bear their iniquities" (Isaiah 53:11).

We must not despise the day of small things. Though it appears to us that little is achieved we must remember that with the Lord one day is as a thousand years. God is working out his purposes and they will not fail. The plummet is in the hands of the heavenly Zerubbabel and the building work is progressing even if only a stone or two are laid in our lifetime. Every stone adds to the building. We are encouraged to be, "stedfast, unmoveable, always abounding in the work of the Lord, forasmuch as ye know that your labour is not in vain in the Lord" (1 Corinthians 15:58). Anything done for the Lord is worthwhile. It is "not in vain."

We are then told of the seven which is interpreted as "the eyes of the Lord, which run to and fro through the whole earth." What are these seven? Again, the Book of Revelation is helpful. In the introduction we find the words: "Grace be unto you, and peace, from him which is, and which was, and which is to come; and from the seven Spirits which are before his throne; And from Jesus Christ, who is the faithful witness, and the first begotten of the dead" (Revelation 1:4-5). Here the three persons of the Trinity are referred to and the Holy Spirit is called the seven Spirits before His throne. God's Spirit works on earth applying redemption to God's people, striving with sinners and sanctifying and equipping the Lord's people for their work. With the aid of the Spirit great things are done.

6. An Unlimited Supply of Blessing (vv11-14)

"Then answered I, and said unto him, What are these two olive trees upon the right side of the candlestick and upon the left side thereof? And I answered again, and said unto him, What be these two olive branches which through the two golden pipes empty the golden oil out of themselves? And he answered me and said, Knowest

thou not what these be? And I said, No, my lord. Then said he, These are the two anointed ones, that stand by the Lord of the whole earth."

The lampstand in the tabernacle had to be filled with oil each morning, but this one received a constant supply of oil from the two olive trees. Because of this it constantly shines and gives its light. But what do the two trees represent? They are described as the "two anointed ones, that stand by the Lord of the whole earth." The word "anointed" refers to the Messiah in the Hebrew of the Old Testament or the Christ in the Greek of the New Testament. The reference here is clearly to Christ as the source of the oil. His atoning work earned this for His church. Paul tells the Ephesians, "When he ascended up on high, he led captivity captive, and gave gifts unto men" (Ephesians 4:8). When Christ ascended, He sent the Holy Spirit, the Comforter, to abide with the church and equip her for her ministry. Oil is often used as a picture of the Spirit. But why are there two anointed ones rather than just one? The two anointed ones at that time were Zerubbabel the governor and Joshua the High Priest. They were types of Christ, and so this refers to the offices of Christ. He was anointed a King and a Priest. He also has the office of prophet but prophets were not normally anointed. The Lord Jesus Christ is set before us here as our great Priest and King who has earned for us the ministry of the Holy Spirit who is the Comforter, the Encourager, the Advocate and the Empowerer. The Spirit is God with us. Praise be to the Lord Jesus Christ who earned salvation for us and the mighty work of the Spirit.

CHAPTER 7

SIXTH VISION: THE FLYING SCROLL

(Zechariah 5:1-4)

The first five visions of Zechariah are full of encouragement but the next two are more challenging. We all need encouragement but we also need rebuke and correction. Too many ministers today flatter their congregations. They tell them that all is well when it is not. They do not mention sin and repentance though these topics are a huge part of the biblical message. People like to hear that God is love, but they forget that His love is a holy love. He created a world that was perfect and happy but very quickly man sinned and so spoiled God's beautiful world. God, in His wrath, cast our first parents out of the Garden of Eden and threatened them with eternal hell if they would not repent and put their trust in the Saviour He provided. The same truth is emphasised when God destroyed the ancient world with a flood, but provided an ark for salvation. Later, God delivered His chosen Israel from bondage in Egypt but, when they sinned in the wilderness, He punished them severely. Only two men, of the many who left Egypt, entered the Promised Land. The rest perished in the desert. Down through the centuries, God sent prophet after prophet to warn the Israelites of their sins but they hated the faithful prophets because they demanded repentance. God complained through Isaiah: "This is a rebellious people, lying children, children that will not hear the law of the Lord: which say to the seers, See not; and to the prophets, Prophesy not unto us right things, speak unto us smooth things, prophesy deceits" (Isaiah 30:9-10). People do not like criticism but always want "smooth things," encouraging and comforting words. However, the faithful messenger will cry like Ezekiel, "Turn ye, turn ye from your evil ways; for why will ye die, O house of Israel?" (Ezekiel 33:11). Continue as you are going and you will perish. Repent and you will be saved.

The teaching of the New Testament is just the same as that of the Old Testament. John the Baptist prepared the way for the Messiah proclaiming, "Repent ye: for the kingdom of heaven is at hand" (Matthew 3:2). When Jesus Christ appeared, He used the same words, "Repent: for the kingdom of heaven is at hand" (Matthew 4:17). Peter on the day of Pentecost, having pointed out the terrible sin of the Jews in crucifying Christ, exhorted the thousands who were listening, "Repent, and be baptized every one of you in the name of Jesus Christ for the remission of sins, and ye shall receive the gift of the Holy Ghost" (Acts 2:38). Paul addressing the Greeks, the philosophers on Mars Hill in Athens, did not use "smooth" words but faithfully declared that God, "now commandeth all men every where to repent: because he hath appointed a day, in the which he will judge the world in righteousness by that man whom he hath ordained; whereof he hath given assurance unto all men, in that he hath raised him from the dead" (Acts 17:30-31). The Bible's message from Genesis to Revelation is clear, but modern man does not want to hear it and sadly too many ministers are afraid to proclaim it. Even most professing Christians today cannot stand hearing their sinful lives condemned. But sin is a terrible reality. Unless we repent, we will perish forever in hell. But the glad tidings of the Gospel are that God has provided a Saviour, His own Son who died on the cross to save sinners. All who repent and receive the Saviour will be reconciled to God, adopted into His family, sanctified, and spend their eternity with Him in His home in heaven. Only holy people get to heaven (Hebrews 12:14).

1. A Flying Scroll (vv1-2)

"Then I turned, and lifted up mine eyes, and looked, and behold a flying roll. And he said unto me, What seest thou? And I answered, I see a flying roll; the length thereof is twenty cubits, and the breadth thereof ten cubits."

Books in ancient times were not bound as ours are today. Rather, they were rolled up in the form of a scroll with a stick attached to each end. Sometimes they were made of leather and other times of papyrus. As they were read they would be unrolled just enough for a person to read them. By unrolling one end and rolling the other end, the whole scroll or book could be read. Normally such books would only be about 25 centimetres or 10 inches broad. This scroll however is enormous. Its length is twenty cubits or 30 feet, or 9.25 metres. Its breadth is 10 cubits, or 15 feet, or 4.5 metres. This gigantic scroll could not be held by one man, nor is it spread on a table but in reality is flying in the air. It is like a banner unfurled by an aeroplane. Interestingly the dimensions are the same as for the holy place in the tabernacle. This emphasises that it is of significance for God's covenant people. Also, it is of the same dimensions as Solomon's porch where the law was read. On this scroll is written a message from God. It is God's word to Judah. We are to ask what is God's word to us today.

2. The Curse (v.3)

"Then said he unto me, This is the curse that goeth forth over the face of the whole earth: for every one that stealeth shall be cut off as on this side according to it; and every one that sweareth shall be cut off as on that side according to it."

The one speaking here is the angel who was showing Zechariah these visions. He explains that the curse goes over the face of the earth. We live in a world where we are constantly hearing cursing and swearing. Some people cannot speak without every second word being a curse. This is of course totally wrong but is nothing new. Jesus confronted it in His own day. Though the Jews were a very religious society yet their language was far from what it should have been. In the Sermon on the Mount our Lord said, "Swear not at all; neither by heaven; for it is God's throne: Nor by the earth; for it is his footstool: neither by Jerusalem; for it is the city of the great King. Neither shalt thou swear by thy head, because thou canst not make one hair white or black. But let your communication be, Yea, yea; Nay, nay: for whatsoever is more than these cometh of evil" (Matthew 5:34-37). All coarse language should be avoided and all swearing is strictly forbidden. The Christian's language should mark him out as different from the world around him. Also remember that the curses of our fellow man can do us no harm, no matter how horrible they sound. God's curses, however, are totally different. They are terrible because God is powerful and what He says happens. Whom God curses is cursed. His wrath and curse must be avoided at all costs. We should greatly fear offending God. As the men of Bethshemesh said: "Who is able to stand before this holy Lord God?" (1 Samuel 6:20).

This huge scroll contains curses upon the one who breaks God's commandments. It is a flying scroll and therefore quick to deliver its punishments. It hovers like a hawk or eagle about to dive upon its prey. "Wheresoever the carcase is, there will the eagles be gathered together" (Matthew 24:28). How frightening for the sinner! How wonderful it is that as Christians we can hide in Christ. He bore the wrath and curse of God for us, being made a curse for us (Galatians 3:13). He is our hiding place (Psalm 32:7). He is a willing Saviour ready to receive and deliver all those who come to Him. He grieved and wept over the Jews' rejection of Him: "O Jerusalem, Jerusalem, thou that killest the prophets, and stonest them which are sent unto thee, how often would I have gathered thy children together, even as a hen gathereth her chickens under her wings, and ye would not!" (Matthew 23:37). All who come to Him are safe under His outstretched wings.

When the Israelites entered the Promised Land they were to be divided into two groups. Half of them would stand upon Mount Gerizim and pronounce blessings. The other half would stand upon Mount Nebo and pronounce curses. Notice some of these curses: "Cursed be the man that maketh any graven or molten image, an abomination unto the Lord, the work of the hands of the craftsman, and putteth it in a secret place. And all the people shall answer and say, Amen. Cursed be he that setteth light by his father or his mother. And all the people shall say, Amen. Cursed be he that removeth his neighbour's landmark. And all the people shall say, Amen. Cursed be he that maketh the blind to wander out of the way. And all the people shall say, Amen. Cursed be he that perverteth the judgment of the stranger, fatherless, and widow. And all the people shall say, Amen" (Deuteronomy 27:15-19). There are many more curses. In the next chapter,

71

Deuteronomy 28, Moses pronounced God's blessings on obedience but he also declared: "It shall come to pass, if thou wilt not hearken unto the voice of the Lord thy God, to observe to do all his commandments and his statutes which I command thee this day; that all these curses shall come upon thee, and overtake thee: Cursed shalt thou be in the city, and cursed shalt thou be in the field. Cursed shall be thy basket and thy store. Cursed shall be the fruit of thy body, and the fruit of thy land, the increase of thy kine, and the flocks of thy sheep. Cursed shalt thou be when thou comest in, and cursed shalt thou be when thou goest out. The Lord shall send upon thee cursing, vexation, and rebuke, in all that thou settest thine hand unto for to do, until thou be destroyed, and until thou perish quickly; because of the wickedness of thy doings, whereby thou hast forsaken me." (Deuteronomy 28:15-20). And the curses continue in that chapter. They are horrible and terrifying.

God's law is serious. He is a great God. Our duty is to obey Him. We were created to "glorify and enjoy Him" (*Westminster Shorter Catechism*, Answer 1). He is a loving God but He is also a holy and just God. He revealed Himself to Moses as: "The Lord, The Lord God, merciful and gracious, longsuffering, and abundant in goodness and truth, Keeping mercy for thousands, forgiving iniquity and transgression and sin, and that will by no means clear the guilty; visiting the iniquity of the fathers upon the children, and upon the children's children, unto the third and to the fourth generation" (Exodus 34:6-7). Sin will certainly be punished. God's name and character demand it. This is emphasised by Paul when he wrote quoting from the Law: "Cursed is every one that continueth not in all things which are written in the book of the law to do them" (Galatians 3:10). It is not simply the big commandments which must be kept. All commandments must be observed in every detail and one breaking of one of the least commandments will send that guilty person to hell forever. God requires perfection: "Be ye therefore perfect, even as your Father which is in heaven is perfect" (Matthew 5:48). None of us is perfect. This is why we need a Saviour.

3. The Punishment (v4)

"I will bring it forth, saith the Lord of hosts, and it shall enter into the house of the thief, and into the house of him that sweareth falsely by my name: and it shall remain in the midst of his house, and shall consume it with the timber thereof and the stones thereof."

Two commandments are singled out as examples but all are included. The Eighth Commandment states, "Thou shalt not steal" (Exodus 20:15). In a sense all the commandments could be summed up under this one. The First Commandment states that we are to have no other gods before Him. To have another God, would be to steal glory from the only real God. The Second states that we are not to worship Him with images or any other way that He Himself has not directed. To do so would again be stealing from the proper worship which is to be afforded to God. The Third Commandment warns against taking God's name in vain which would again be stealing from the honour which should be given to God. The Fourth Commandment requires that we give to God one day in seven to be specially kept for Him as a holy day. Not to do so would be to steal the time for our pleasure which we should give to God. The Fifth Commandment calls upon us to honour our parents. Failure to do so steals from them the respect they are due. The Sixth Commandment condemns murder and the stealing of another person's life from them. The Seventh Commandment condemns adultery or the stealing of someone else's wife. The Ninth Commandment condemns the stealing of the truth from another person. The Tenth Commandment, which is "Thou shalt not covet", makes plain that even the desire to have what belongs to someone else is a sin because it is stealing in the heart and it is the thought that precedes every other stealing. The very first sin of Adam and Even was stealing fruit from God's special tree. Stealing is a very serious sin.

The other sin mentioned here is swearing falsely. This is also to commit a great crime against the Lord. To swear falsely means taking God's name in vain and so breaking the Third Commandment. It also means bearing false witness or telling a lie which is a direct breach of the Ninth

73

Commandment. To sin in this way involves treating God with contempt. It calls the God who is almighty and all-seeing to witness a statement made. Further it requires God to punish if that promise is broken. To go ahead and break a promise in the light of this is to regard God as not seeing what is happening on the earth, or not caring what happens, or not able to punish a breach of promise. It is not loving God with all your heart and soul and strength and mind. Indeed, it is despising Him and His rule over the earth. Swearing falsely also involves not loving your neighbour but trying to deceive and so hurt him. There is a particularly serious warning attached to the third commandment. "The Lord will not hold him guiltless that taketh his name in vain" (Exodus 20:7).

The great Scroll is threatening. It is flying, watching like a hawk, hovering as it were over the sinner, ready to pounce. God has His eye on every individual in the world and on all that is happening. The scroll enters the house of the transgressor and burns up the stones as well as the timber. When the Jews returned from their exile they had permission of the emperor to rebuild the temple at Jerusalem. The Samaritans opposed the work and succeeded in stopping it for a time. Later it was discovered that the Jews had the emperor's permission and in fact Darius decreed, "That whosoever shall alter this word, let timber be pulled down from his house, and being set up, let him be hanged thereon; and let his house be made a dunghill for this. And the God that hath caused his name to dwell there destroy all kings and people, that shall put to their hand to alter and to destroy this house of God which is at Jerusalem. I, Darius have made a decree; let it be done with speed" (Ezra 6:11-12). Terrible punishment would come on any who opposed Darius' decree. But far worse will happen to the one who is found guilty here. The scroll of curses would enter their house and remain there. Not only was the timber of the house to be burnt but even the very stones were to be consumed. This is the sort of fire that came down from heaven on the altar which Elijah built on Mount Carmel. Everything was burnt. God promises blessing on the faithful, but He hates sin and will surely punish it with terrifying wrath. So, we see that the great scroll has God's law written upon it, and the curse of God upon the law breakers. It will destroy all who are outside of Christ.

In conclusion, we should note that there are three uses of the law of God. First, God's law shows us our sin, convicting us of our sinfulness and danger so that we flee to Christ as our only hope for salvation. The law, as Paul said, is our schoolmaster to bring us to Christ (Galatians 3:24). It is binding upon every man and woman. To some extent it is written upon every conscience and is the basis for God's judgment on the last day: "They were judged every man according to their works" (Revelation 20:13). The second use of the law is as a rule for society. It provides a basis for the laws of every country and in this way restrains evil. The third use of the law is as a guide and rule for the Christian life. Jesus said, "If ye love me, keep my commandments" (John 14:15). Having been saved by grace we need the law as a lamp to our feet and a light to our path. We do not merit salvation by keeping the commandments but by keeping the commandments we show our love and appreciation to God. The law, like the Scroll here, is what will condemn the unbelieving sinner to hell. So, this vision is a warning against sin and its consequences.

CHAPTER 8

SEVENTH VISION: THE EPHAH

(Zechariah 5:5-11)

In the Sixth Vision the prophet saw a flying scroll which contained curses upon the wicked. Sin is certainly going to be punished. This scroll entered the house of the thief and the perjurer and burns all up, even the very stones of their home. God's wrath will burn against the wicked with fire unquenchable through all the ages of eternity. This present vision is similar. People seem to sin with impunity. They appear to get off with their sin but, we are assured, eventually all sin will be punished. "The wages of sin is death" (Romans 6:23) and God never fails to pay wages. Sin is serious. God hates it. The wicked shall not go unpunished.

1. The Ephah (vv5-6)

"Then the angel that talked with me went forth, and said unto me, Lift up now thine eyes, and see what is this that goeth forth. And I said, What is it? And he said, This is an ephah that goeth forth. He said moreover, This is their resemblance through all the earth."

The same angel who had shown him the previous visions directs Zechariah to notice a new revelation. The prophet is still thinking about the previous vision but there is now another vision to see. He sees an ephah. An ephah was a measuring basket used for selling grain. Among the main crops grown in Israel were cereals, wheat and barley. Merchants would use these baskets to measure the quantities being sold. Idolatry used to be the big sin of the Israelites. Time and time again they forsook the Lord and turned to the gods of the nations round about them. Shortly after leaving Egypt they made a golden calf and worshipped it. Later in the plains of Moab they were enticed by beautiful Midianite and Moabite women to come to their pagan feasts in honour of their idols and commit fornication with them. After entering the Promised Land and after the death of Joshua and the elders who outlived Joshua, they forget the Lord and turn to worship Balaam. God hands them over to their enemies who oppress them. In their suffering they turn to the Lord who raises up a deliverer for them. Again, they fall away and again, in their trouble, they cry to God and He saves them. The Book of Judges records how time and time again they backslide and worship idols. Their enemies are allowed to conquer them and oppress them. In their distress they return to God and He sends them a judge to deliver them. The same is true in the days of the kings. Eventually God hands them over to the Babylonians who carry them away captive to Babylon. For seventy years they suffer exile far from home. By the time, eventually, when they return to the land of Canaan, they are at last cured of this kind of gross idolatry. But, sadly, new sins emerge. Now their sins are the love of money, materialism and self-righteousness.

When they first returned from Babylon, they set up the altar of the Lord, and began again to worship God with the sacrifices which He had required of Moses and Aaron. They also started to rebuild the temple and were initially enthusiastic. But gradually, struggling with the difficulties, facing the opposition of enemies, but especially concerned to build their own homes and cultivate their own fields, they left off the building work. They procrastinated, putting off the building of the temple. They said one day they would build it but not now. Haggai refers to this in his prophecy: "This people say, The time is not come, the time that the Lord's house should be built. Then came the word of the Lord by Haggai the prophet, saying, Is it time for you, O ye, to dwell in your cieled houses, and this house lie waste? Now therefore thus saith the Lord of hosts; Consider your ways. Ye have sown much, and bring in little; ye eat, but ye have not enough; ye drink, but ye are not filled with drink; ye clothe you, but there is none warm; and he that earneth wages earneth wages to put it into a bag with holes. Thus saith the Lord of hosts; Consider your ways" (Haggai 1:2-7). They lived in their beautiful ceiled or panelled house while God's house was a ruin. They worked hard to be rich but, in reality, they were not prospering. They earned money as it were to put it into a purse with a hole in the bottom. Their money just disappeared. There was no blessing on their labours. Jesus said: "Seek ye first the kingdom of God, and his righteousness; and all these things shall be added unto you" (Matthew 6:33). In this we have a wonderful promise. But because they were seeking first their own wealth God refused to bless them with prosperity in earthly riches.

The sin of the Jews at that time was exactly the same as the sins of the world today. People's priorities are wealth and material things. The majority are full of covetousness. In their greed they forget that they have souls and spend almost all their time and energy in the pursuit of riches. Paul warned, "The love of money is the root of all evil: which while some coveted after, they have erred from the faith, and pierced themselves through with many sorrows. But thou, O man of God, flee these things; and follow after righteousness, godliness, faith, love, patience, meekness" (1 Timothy 6:10-11). Strikes are common as people demand more pay. People move far away for a better paying job and never seem to ask will I be near a good church, or will it badly affect my opportunity to serve in God's church, or will the longer hours I have to work have a negative effect upon my soul? Jesus warned: "You cannot serve God and mammon" (Matthew 6:24).

2. The Woman (vv7-8)

"And, behold, there was lifted up a talent of lead: and this is a woman that sitteth in the midst of the ephah. And he said, This is wickedness. And he cast it into the midst of the ephah; and he cast the weight of lead upon the mouth thereof."

Zechariah next sees a woman sitting in the middle of the basket. The lid has been raised. The basket seems too small for her and she appears to be trying to get out of it. She is called wickedness and represents the Jewish people. The wickedness is obviously connected with the ephah or measure used in buying and selling. We think of God's words through Amos: "Hear this, O ye that swallow up the needy, even to make the poor of the land to fail, saying, When will the new moon be gone, that we may sell corn? and the sabbath, that we may set forth wheat, making the ephah small, and the shekel great, and falsifying the balances by deceit? That we may buy the poor for silver, and the needy for a pair of shoes; yea, and sell the refuse of the wheat?" (Amos 8:4-6). There are many sins particularly connected to the market place. God sees the greed that oppresses the poor. He notices when the ephah for selling is made smaller than it should be and the shekel for payment made larger. He is aware of the wicked hearts of the merchants who grudge stopping their work for holy days and giving the new moon and the Sabbath to God. They long for the holy days to be past so that they can return to their dealings and their money-making.

Similarly, God warns through the prophet Micah that He will certainly punish the cheating merchants: "Are there yet the treasures of wickedness in the house of the wicked, and the scant measure that is abominable? Shall I count them pure with the wicked balances, and with the bag of deceitful weights? For the rich men thereof are full of violence, and the inhabitants thereof have spoken lies, and their tongue is deceitful in their mouth. Therefore also will I make thee sick in smiting thee, in making thee desolate because of thy sins" (Micah 6:10-13). They had a bag of deceitful weights which were used to deceive and rob people. The dishonest traders are becoming rich but God is watching. Nothing is hidden from Him. He sees their behaviour as abominable. He will smite them and make them sick and desolate.

Our Lord was troubled when He saw the Court of the Gentiles in the temple, which was meant to be a place for prayer for the Gentiles, taken over by the money-changers and merchants who were selling their sheep and cattle and doves. At a cost they had received permission from the priests to trade there, and the animals and birds which they sold would be approved for sacrifices. The priests were paid bribes to allow it and so made money out of it and the merchants got their profits too. "And Jesus went into the temple of God, and cast out all them that sold and bought in the temple, and overthrew the tables of the moneychangers, and the seats of them that sold doves, And said unto them, It is written, My house shall be called the house of prayer; but ye have made it a den of thieves" (Matthew

21:12-13). There is of course no sin in being a merchant nor in being rich. Sadly, however the love of money led many of these Jews into dishonesty. They could easily find ways to justify making a little extra "profit." After cheating two or three times the conscience is hardened and no longer condemns. An unconverted person dead in trespasses and sins can easily degenerate into being a thief. Even born-again Christians must be constantly on guard against the temptations of Satan. What a sad picture we have here of God's church in Old Testament times. She is represented by a woman called wickedness sitting in a measuring basket.

3. The Weight of Lead (vv7-8)

"And, behold, there was lifted up a talent of lead: and this is a woman that sitteth in the midst of the ephah. And he said, This is wickedness. And he cast it into the midst of the ephah; and he cast the weight of lead upon the mouth thereof."

It appears as if the woman is trying to get out of the basket. She is pushing up the lid. But a huge lead weight is placed upon her crushing her down. The world and the devil promise freedom and pleasure. If you have lots of money, they say you will have a really happy life. People work very hard, and for long hours, and sometimes in difficult and unpleasant employment in order to be rich. Some, foolishly, put their hard-earned money into the lottery hoping for sudden wealth. If they win, they think that will be the end of all their troubles. They will be able to enjoy themselves. But it does not work that way. Money like the devil is a cruel master. The more money you have the more worries it brings. It is Christ alone who gives joy and peace and lasting happiness. He is the one who sets us free: "Then said Jesus to those Jews which believed on him, If ye continue in my word, then are ye my disciples indeed; And ye shall know the truth, and the truth shall make you free" (John 8:31-32).

4. Carried Away (vv9-11)

"Then lifted I up mine eyes, and looked, and, behold, there came out two women, and the wind was in their wings; for they had wings like the wings of a stork: and

they lifted up the ephah between the earth and the heaven. Then said I to the angel that talked with me, Whither do these bear the ephah? And he said unto me, To build it an house in the land of Shinar: and it shall be established, and set there upon her own base."

Two women now appear having wings like a stork and the wind is in their wings. The stork is a migratory bird with strong wings and able to fly a great distance. These women come and pick up the basket with the wicked woman inside it and carry it far away to the land of Shinar. Shinar first appears in Genesis 11 as the place where an attempt was made to build the tower of Babel that would reach right up to heaven. That was man in determined revolt against God. That too was where Babylon was located. The Jews have just returned from seventy years exile in Babylon. This speaks of a new exile. Four hundred years later the sin of the Jews had reached a new climax with the rejection and crucifixion of the Messiah whom God sent to them. When Pilate tried to release Jesus, whom he knew to be innocent of the charges laid against Him, the Jews said the Jews said "His blood be on us, and [up]on our children" (Matthew 27:25). The Roman eagles came. A terrible struggle ensued and many died in the siege, the famine and the war. The Jews who were left were carried off to a new exile that has lasted for 2000 years. Only now are they returning to their own land once more.

The ephah was set upon its own base. It was not founded on Christ or on the truth but on their own righteousness. The Jews are notorious for their self-righteousness and arrogance. They think because they are Jews and keep their traditions that they have favour with God. But by rejecting the God-appointed Messiah they are under God's condemnation. Yet surely in their return at last to their own land we see the Lord's mercy reaching them after so many years. They were God's chosen people and the gifts and calling of God are without repentance. "And they also, if they abide not still in unbelief, shall be grafted in: for God is able to graft them in again. For if thou wert cut out of the olive tree which is wild by nature, and wert grafted contrary to nature into a good olive tree: how much more shall these, which be the natural branches, be grafted into their own olive tree? For I would not, brethren, that ye should be ignorant of this mystery, lest ye should be wise in your own conceits; that blindness in part is happened to Israel, until the fulness of the Gentiles be come in. And so all Israel shall be saved: as it is written, There shall come out of Sion the Deliverer, and shall turn away ungodliness from Jacob" (Romans 11:23-26).

So here again there is a call to repent of our sins and to return to the Lord. We are warned against the love of money and called upon to set our hearts on heavenly and eternal things rather than on worldly things. If we continue to love this world and its riches and pleasures God's wrath will break out upon us.

CHAPTER 9

EIGHTH VISION: GOD REIGNS!

(Zechariah 6:1-8)

The church today appears very weak. Huge forces are arrayed against it. Satan is always very busy. He hates God and all that belongs to God. He tries all he can do to hurt the cause of God. He wants to undermine the glory of God. He is the great opponent of the church of God. The over-riding ambition of his life is to lead astray the people of God and he uses all his followers and all his resources to achieve that end. He is highly intelligent. He is of great experience. He has been learning his trade ever since the fall of man. He knows what is likely to work and he never seems to forget. He has thousands of demons at his command and also millions of wicked men who are his slaves.

In addition, inside every born-again Christian there is the flesh. This is the remains of corruption, sometimes called fallen human nature. It is indwelling sin which Paul describes as a "law in my members, warring against the law of my mind, and bringing me into captivity to the law of sin which is in my members" (Romans 7:23). Satan has access to our minds and can play upon our desires and stir up our lusts. We need the whole armour of God to resist him (Ephesians 6:10-20). The church today is weak because Christians are so busy working, caring for their families and enjoying the many pleasures which are freely available. God's people are not looking after the health of their souls and forget that they are in a war and that they have powerful enemies who are determined to destroy them. Paul also warned elsewhere: "We wrestle not against flesh and blood, but against principalities, against powers, against the rulers of the darkness of this world, against spiritual wickedness in high places" (Ephesians 6:12). Christ sent us forth to spread the kingdom by the preaching of the gospel and so bringing the world into subjection to Him. Our concern is to save men and women from hell but Satan is busy opposing us.

In days gone by, almost everyone believed in a Creator who made this world and man upon it. This meant that people generally believed in God as the Judge before whom we would all one day have to stand to give our account for our lives. On the basis of this judgment there was a heaven or a hell in the next life. But today many believe in the "Big Bang" as that which formed the world in the first place, and evolution as that which produced man. It seems strange that out of nothing there should be a bang which brings a universe into existence. Also, when one notes the wonderful complexity of the simplest form of life, it is amazing that scientists should believe in the spontaneous generation of living organisms. And then also to believe that, by means of little steps, man would eventually evolve from these single-cell creatures. In point of fact, there would have to be so many huge and impossible steps to produce such body parts as eyes, ears, a heart with warm blood as opposed to cold blooded creatures and sexual organs in creatures which originally reproduced asexually. Yet many are happy to believe in this because the only alternative is to believe in the Creator God to whom they are responsible. Evolution helps them to get rid of God and quietens their consciences which warn them that one day they will be judged. The universities, the schools and the media unite in proclaiming that there is no God. Evolution is taken as a fact and those who do not believe in it are laughed out of court. This creates a huge resistance to the preaching of the gospel. Sadly, many churches also accept evolution, rejecting the teaching of the Bible, and so help to undermine the gospel demands. Secular thinking which has no place for God has taken over our society. People are constantly told that they must keep their religion to themselves as a private matter of beliefs and practices. Post-modernism teaches that one man's religion is as good as the next. King Charles spoke of himself as a defender of all faiths including the faith of humanists. So, in the eyes of many today there is no such thing as objective truth in the realm of religion.

Another powerful force in the world today is the *sexual revolution*. The 1960s pop culture undermined marriage. Contraceptives and abortion allowed women to freely engage in sexual activity with multiple partners without the problem of children being born. The Bible teaches that sex is to be practised only within marriage, and that marriage should only be between a man and a woman and to be for life. The God-ordained family has been undermined. Premarital sex has become the norm. Many never marry and, even when they do, divorce is very common. The internet promotes pornography on a massive scale and many see no fault in it. Homosexual practices have become acceptable. Now transgenderism confuses many of our teenagers. Our society can see no sin of a sexual kind except paedophilia and one wonders how long it will be till that is also acceptable. Christians who take a stand for biblical sexual ethics are mocked as 'old-fashioned' and, indeed, hateful. They are persecuted, if they will not affirm the immoral choices of their neighbours.

Sadly, many of the churches, especially the large mainline church, seem to see their role as simply to reflect what is acceptable in society in general. They were affected by higher criticism in the nineteenth century. This taught that the Bible had errors in it and therefore could not be fully trusted. Human reason is the standard and not divine revelation. There are no such things as miracles or prophecy. The Bible is simply man's reflections about God and religion. Indeed, the Bible is treated as just one book among many. It is regarded as having no special authority. All its statements can be challenged by human reason. Churches generally became centres for social work and left-wing politics. The churches prophetic voice was lost.

Today there is great spiritual apathy. Only a tiny proportion of the population attend a church. When Christians preach on the streets or try to engage their neighbours in conversation about their souls and their need to repent and believe the gospel, they are met either with a yawn or with hostility. Few are willing to listen to what the evangelical church has to say and the liberal church has no gospel message. In this situation the prophecy which we have here Zechariah chapter 6 is highly relevant and provides great encouragement.

1. The Four Chariots (vv1-3)

"And I turned, and lifted up mine eyes, and looked, and, behold, there came four chariots out from between two mountains; and the mountains were mountains of brass. In the first chariot were red horses; and in the second chariot black horses; And in the third chariot white horses; and in the fourth chariot grisled and bay horses."

This eighth vision is similar to the first in which the horsemen go forth and survey the earth. The chariots here are carrying out the purposes of God. Both convey the idea that God reigns. He is the Sovereign who rules in the affairs of men and women. Nothing happens but according to His will and plan. The intervening visions between the first and this eighth one have been dealing with Israel's own relationship with God.

It is interesting to note that the chariots go out between mountains of brass. They go out from the presence of the Lord. The Lord dwells in His temple. The temple of Solomon had two great pillars of brass at its entrance, one called Jachin and the other Boaz. These pillars have now become mountains. This speaks of strength, durability, and protection. God dwells in His holy place and from there He rules the nations. Men and devils are in rebellion against Him, but they can make no impression on the great mountains of brass. Satan's fiery darts fall harmlessly. Christ said: "I will build my church; and the gates of hell will not prevail against it" (Matthew 16:18). Man's godless philosophy, his humanism, his immorality, his secularism, his cultural Marxism and his blasphemy make no impression on God. "Why do the heathen rage, and the people imagine a vain thing? The kings of the earth set themselves, and the rulers take counsel together, against the Lord, and against his anointed, saying, Let us break their bands asunder, and cast away their cords from us. He that sitteth in the heavens shall laugh: the Lord shall have them in derision. Then shall he speak unto them in his wrath, and vex them in his sore displeasure" (Psalm 2:1-5). How important it is to keep this vision of the Almighty before our eyes. God is in control. He is not in a panic. He sits. He watches and laughs as puny men and devils plot rebellion against Him. When His time comes, and when He sees fit, He will speak in wrath and pour upon them His fiery indignation. None can resist His will. His enemies will become His footstool and the footstool of His people. "The God of peace shall bruise Satan under your feet shortly" (Romans 16:20). We are on the winning side. Fear not man whose breath is in his nostrils (Isaiah 2:22). "We are more than conquerors through him that loved us" (Romans 8:37).

Chariots in ancient times were a bit like tanks today. They are powerful symbols of war. Here there are four chariots. This speaks of the four corners of the earth. God's rule is universal. No part of the earth is exempt from His control. In the words of the Psalmist, "The chariots of God are twenty thousand, even thousands of angels: the Lord is among them, as in Sinai, in the holy place" (Psalm 68:17). God reigns and none can stand against Him. His armies are immense. His purposes will certainly be carried out.

The colours of the horses are symbolic. Red horses speak of war and bloodshed. In fact, God is involved in every war. It is not chance or fate that causes war. From our viewpoint it seems like megalomaniacs invade other countries and want to rule over them. We look at powerful men like Putin today or Hitler in the past, but in reality God is in control. God sends war. Putin is His servant. This of course does not justify Putin's cruel war. Putin at the end of the day will have to answer to God for all the carnage and suffering he caused. But it is God's red horses which march through Ukraine. We might worry about the break out of nuclear war, but none can press the nuclear button except as God wills it. What a comfort it is to know that God controls the chariots of war!

Black horses speak of mourning and death. Death is universal in this world. There is for all of us "a time to be born, and a time to die" (Ecclesiastes 3:2). Our lives are in God's hands and He has set the exact moment of our birth and death. How important it is for us to prepare for death. It will soon come to us all. "It is appointed unto men once to die, but after this the judgment" (Hebrews 9:27). We live our lives before God and one day, at His appointed time, our soul and body will be separated and, if we are wicked, we will open our eyes in hell and, if we are righteous, we will open our eyes in heaven. In every death God is calling men and women to give their account to Him.

The white horses speak of victory. Nothing can thwart God's plan. He carries out His purposes to their conclusion. God will eventually usher in the new heavens and the new earth wherein dwells righteousness. The colour of the horses in the final chariot are more difficult to translate. Here we have the term 'grisled'. Others translate it as *piebald*. It would seem to be a mixture of colours. The term "bay horses" is translated by some as strong horses. The essential truth conveyed by the vision is that God rules the nations and the different colours represent the different conditions found on the earth. Those building the temple meet with different challenges but God will enable them to overcome them all.

2. The Four Spirits sent (vv4-8)

"Then I answered and said unto the angel that talked with me, What are these, my lord? And the angel answered and said unto me, These are the four spirits of the heavens, which go forth from standing before the Lord of all the earth. The black horses which are therein go forth into the north country; and the white go forth after them; and the grisled go forth toward the south country. And the bay went forth, and sought to go that they might walk to and fro through the earth: and he said, Get you hence, walk to and fro through the earth. So they walked to and fro through the earth. Then cried he upon me, and spake unto me, saying, Behold, these that go toward the north country have quieted my spirit in the north country."

The prophet asks the angel to explain. In Hebrew the word for spirit and for wind is the same. These four chariots are the four spirits of God, the four messengers of God, or the four winds of God. They go forth at His command. They do not simply roam over Israel but over the whole earth. They go through the lands of the Muslims, the Hindus the Buddhists and the atheists. None escape their attention. God reigns over all the earth, indeed over the whole universe, and heaven and hell too.

GOD REIGNS!

The black horses go forth to the north country. The white go forth after them insuring complete victory. This is the direction from which the great enemies of Israel came, Assyria and Babylon. The black horses spell death to these enemies of God's people. Babylon was a great city but the time came when it was destroyed. It was a proud city and would have laughed at the words of the Jewish prophet if they heard them. As one commentator (T. V. Moore) put it, "Now the winds whistle through the reeds of the Euphrates, where Babylon then sat in her pride; and loneliness, desolation and death are stationed there the sentinel witnesses of the truth that His words do not return to Him void, that His spirit is quieted in the land of the north." Babylon's destruction was total and to this very day it is a ruin. President Saddam Hussein planned to rebuild it, but he too was destroyed. The grisled went to the south country, that is Egypt, another old enemy. Wave after wave of desolation passed over that once mighty land of pyramids, sphinxes and temples, now just a shadow of her former glory.

The bay went out patrolling the whole world again sent by God and carrying out His will. God rules the nations. He raises up one and casts another down. Those that went to the north country quieted God's spirit in the North. The Chaldeans had been used to chastise God's people but when they had carried out the task God has assigned them, then these enemies of His people were destroyed. God loves His church and will punish all her enemies. Since these days other empires have come and gone, Persia, Greece, Rome, and the more modern ones. But God cares for His church. Through every age He looks after His people and all their enemies will become like the dust under their feet. But the final destruction of all the enemies of God and His people awaits the second coming of Christ when he will return, "In flaming fire taking vengeance on them that know not God, and that obey not the gospel of our Lord Jesus Christ: Who shall be punished with everlasting destruction from the presence of the Lord, and from the glory of his power; When he shall come to be glorified in his saints, and to be admired in all them that believe (because our testimony among you was believed) in that day" (2 Thessalonians 1:8-10).

CHAPTER 10

CLIMAX OF THE VISIONS: THE CROWNING OF JOSHUA

(Zechariah 6:9-15)

In the eighth vision we saw how God actively reigns over the earth and the enemies of the Lord's people will be destroyed. Some have described this new section, Zechariah 6:9-15, as the ninth vision, but it is not a vision as such, but rather a symbolic acting out of a glorious truth. God commands the prophet to perform a symbolic action closely linked to the visions, building upon them and yet focussing the faith of the Lord's people on the coming Messiah. Men and women in Old Testament times were saved by looking forward in faith to the coming Messiah just as we are saved by looking back in faith to our Lord Jesus Christ and His finished work at Calvary. God makes His covenant of grace with men and woman promising eternal life but there is one condition or requirement and that is faith. It goes without saying that we must also remember that faith "is the gift of God" (Ephesians 2:8).

1. Make a Crown (vv9-11)

"And the word of the Lord came unto me, saying, Take of them of the captivity, even of Heldai, of Tobijah, and of Jedaiah, which are come from Babylon, and come thou the same day, and go into the house of Josiah the son of Zephaniah; Then take silver and gold, and make crowns, and set them upon the head of Joshua the son of Josedech, the high priest."

Here God speaks to the prophet. Several men had come from Babylon bringing gold and silver, a collection that had been made, to help with the building of the temple in Jerusalem. Zechariah was instructed to go to the house where the men were lodging and take some of the silver and gold and "make crowns, and set them upon the head of Joshua the son of

Josedech, the high priest" (v11). Some see the plural "crowns" as referring to several rings composing the one crown. However, it is better to see it as a plural of intensity. He was to make a magnificent crown, not some mere token crown. This is emphasised by the fact that the verb used is singular. It was one crown. He was then to place this crown, not on the head of Zerubbabel the governor, but on the head of the high priest Joshua.

This is fascinating. Never before had a high priest reigned in Israel. Neither was a king allowed to act as a priest. When King Uzziah, carried away with his own importance, entered the temple to offer incense he was struck with leprosy (2 Chronicles 26:19). God punished him. But here we have a priest being anointed king. Clearly this is a prophecy of the One who will be both a priest and a king. In the book of Genesis, we are told that Melchizedek had been such a one, as he was "King of Salem ... and he was the priest of the most high God" (Genesis 14:18). The Psalmist prophesied of One coming who would be a king: "The Lord shall send the rod of thy strength out of Zion: rule thou in the midst of thine enemies", and He would also be "a priest for ever after the order of Melchizedek" (Psalm 110:2, 4). The Epistle to the Hebrews explains how this Melchizedek was like the Son of God and so a type of the Messiah: "For this Melchizedek, king of Salem, priest of the most high God, who met Abraham returning from the slaughter of the kings, and blessed him; to whom also Abraham gave a tenth part of all; first being by interpretation King of righteousness, and after that also King of Salem, which is, King of peace; without father, without mother, without descent, having neither beginning of days, nor end of life; but made like unto the Son of God; abideth a priest continually" (Hebrews 7:1-3). Joshua is crowned as a typical or symbolic figure. He represents the Christ who is coming.

It is interesting to note that Joshua was first a priest before he was king. Our Lord Jesus first came and offered Himself as a sacrifice for our sins before He was crowned. It was a once for all time sacrifice on the cross of Calvary: "For by one offering he hath perfected for ever them that are sanctified" (Hebrews 10:14). Following this great priestly act He rose on the third day. Forty days later He ascended up to heaven and was anointed

King as the Epistle to the Hebrews states: "Who being the brightness of his glory, and the express image of his person, and upholding all things by the word of his power, when he had by himself purged our sins, sat down on the right hand of the Majesty on high" and His Father said to Him, "Thy throne, O God, is for ever and ever: a sceptre of righteousness is the sceptre of thy kingdom" (Hebrews 1:3, 8). Paul describes His exaltation which followed His humiliation: "Who, being in the form of God, thought it not robbery to be equal with God: But made himself of no reputation, and took upon him the form of a servant, and was made in the likeness of men: And being found in fashion as a man, he humbled himself, and became obedient unto death, even the death of the cross. Wherefore God also hath highly exalted him, and given him a name which is above every name: That at the name of Jesus every knee should bow, of things in heaven, and things in earth, and things under the earth; And that every tongue should confess that Jesus Christ is Lord, to the glory of God the Father" (Philippians 2:6-11).

Zechariah is prophesying at a low point in the history of Israel. The Jews had just returned from their seventy-year exile in Babylon. They were attempting to resettle in the land of Israel. They were building the temple once more but their resources were few. But here he is telling them that there is a great future ahead. A magnificent crown is placed upon the head of the priest. The Priest whom Joshua symbolised was to be a great King, indeed the King of kings. The coming Messiah would "have dominion also from sea to sea, and from the river unto the ends of the earth. They that dwell in the wilderness shall bow before him; and his enemies shall lick the dust. The kings of Tarshish and of the isles shall bring presents: the kings of Sheba and Seba shall offer gifts. Yea, all kings shall fall down before him: all nations shall serve him" (Psalm 72:8-11). Furthermore, His kingdom shall last forever. It is said of Him: "Thy kingdom is an everlasting kingdom, and thy dominion endureth throughout all generations" (Psalm 145:13). Daniel received a vision of this: "I saw in the night visions, and, behold, one like the Son of man came with the clouds of heaven, and came to the Ancient of days, and they brought him near before him. And there was given him dominion, and glory, and a kingdom, that all people, nations, and languages, should serve him: his dominion is an everlasting dominion, which shall not pass away, and his kingdom that which shall not be destroyed" (Daniel 7:13-14).

What tremendous encouragement this would be to Joshua, Zerubbabel and all God's people as they struggled to build the temple! And what encouragement it is to us as we seek to build God's church today facing many cunning and powerful enemies! We are on the winning side! The Son of Man who is our Saviour, who by His priestly work atoned for our sins, is also the One who will reign for ever and His kingdom will never be destroyed, and we shall sit with Him in His throne and reign with Him (Revelation 3:21).

2. The Branch will build His Temple (vv12-13)

"And speak unto him, saying, Thus speaketh the Lord of hosts, saying, Behold the man whose name is The Branch; and he shall grow up out of his place, and he shall build the temple of the Lord: Even he shall build the temple of the Lord; and he shall bear the glory, and shall sit and rule upon his throne; and he shall be a priest upon his throne: and the counsel of peace shall be between them both."

Zechariah is told to address Joshua with these words from God: "Behold the man whose name is the Branch; and he shall grow up out of his place, and he shall build the temple of the Lord" (v12). The name "The Branch" obviously refers to the one who had already been spoken of in Zechariah 3. He is the Branch of David and He would be the really fruitful Branch. "He shall see his seed" (Isaiah 53:10). They would be as the stars of the sky and as the sand of the seashore for multitude. He is a man and truly a man. "He shall grow out of his place." He shall branch out. There is a play on the word. He would not suddenly appear out of heaven to perform his saving work. He shall grow out of the root of David. Isaiah prophesies concerning Him: "And there shall come forth a rod out of the stem of Jesse, and a Branch shall grow out of his roots: And the spirit of the Lord shall rest upon him, the spirit of wisdom and understanding, the spirit of counsel and might, the spirit of knowledge and of the fear of the Lord;

93

And shall make him of quick understanding in the fear of the Lord: and he shall not judge after the sight of his eyes, neither reprove after the hearing of his ears: But with righteousness shall he judge the poor, and reprove with equity for the meek of the earth: and he shall smite the earth: with the rod of his mouth, and with the breath of his lips shall he slay the wicked. And righteousness shall be the girdle of his loins, and faithfulness the girdle of his reins" (Isaiah 11:1-5).

Born in Bethlehem to the family of David He would grow up in Israel, the great Son of David who was also David's Lord. He would not be a foreigner but one of Israel. He would be anointed with the Spirit of God to enable Him to perform His work. He would show mercy and kindness to the poor and the needy, but eventually He would destroy His enemies in His wrath. In His righteousness He would justify poor sinners who trust in Him but He would judge and condemn proud Pharisees who trust in their own righteousness. His great work will be to build the temple of the Lord. Now Zerubbabel is building the replacement for the temple which Solomon built, but the temple the Branch builds will be a glorious, spiritual temple of an altogether different order.

Jesus said to the Jews: "Destroy this temple, and in three days I will raise it up. Then said the Jews, Forty and six years was this temple in building, and wilt thou rear it up in three days? But he spake of the temple of his body" (John 2:19-21). The Jews were very proud of their temple. It had indeed initially been built by Zerubbabel but then over a period of 46 years was greatly extended and beautified by Herod. They were shocked at what Jesus said. Surely the temple of the Lord would not be destroyed! However, it would not be Jesus who destroyed their temple but they themselves. In their rejection of Jesus the Messiah they destroyed the temple. When Jesus died the all-important veil of the temple that separated the Holy Place from the Holy of Holies where God used to dwell was torn down from top to bottom. Then in AD70 the destruction of the temple was completed. The Jews rebelled against the Romans and the Romans burnt the temple and left not one stone upon another.

THE CROWNING OF JOSHUA

How could Jesus build a new temple in three days? But Jesus was speaking of the temple of his body. "When therefore he was risen from the dead, his disciples remembered that he had said this unto them; and they believed the scripture, and the word which Jesus had said" (John 2:22). The Jews put Him to death but He rose again on the third day. But now a new temple is being built. Christians are the body of Christ, "Now ye are the body of Christ, and members in particular" (1 Corinthians 12:27). Jesus said "I will build my church; and the gates of hell shall not prevail against it" (Matthew 16:18).

Zerubbabel and Joshua were struggling to build the temple but here there is encouragement. The temple will indeed be built, but better still, a far more glorious temple will one day be built. It will be built of living stones. Peter could say, "Ye also, as lively stones, are built up a spiritual house" (1 Peter 2:5). Paul wrote to the Ephesian Christians that they were, "built upon the foundation of the apostles and prophets, Jesus Christ himself being the chief corner stone; in whom all the building fitly framed together groweth unto an holy temple in the Lord: in whom ye also are builded together for an habitation of God through the Spirit" (Ephesians 1:20-22). This temple will remain. In heaven there will be no temple because it is all temple (Revelation 21:22). God will dwell in the midst of His people forever.

It is also said of the One who will build the temple, "He shall bear the glory" (v13). The Jews subjected Him to the greatest humiliation they could imagine; mocked, buffeted, spat on, crucified, buried, but He shall be glorified. God raised Him again. He "shall sit and rule upon his throne; and he shall be a priest upon his throne" (v13). He ascended up to heaven. The Psalmist prophesied: "The Lord said unto my Lord, Sit thou at my right hand, until I make thine enemies thy footstool" (Ps.110:1). Paul wrote, "For he must reign, till he hath put all enemies under his feet. The last enemy that shall be destroyed is death" (1 Corinthians 15:25-26). It is interesting that Zechariah prophesies, "He shall be a priest upon his throne." The priest will become king. Joshua was first a priest before symbolically becoming king. Our Lord Jesus performed His priestly sacrifice before His exaltation and coronation.

3. The Counsel of Peace (v13)

Even he shall build the temple of the Lord; and he shall bear the glory, and shall sit and rule upon his throne; and he shall be a priest upon his throne: and the counsel of peace shall be between them both

Next, we notice these interesting words: "the counsel of peace shall be between them both" (v13). Some interpret this from the immediate context to mean that the counsel of peace is between the priest and the prophet and that there will be no conflict between the two. However, here, obviously the priest and king are the same person so it is very strange to talk of some pact between them. Rather, one should take a step back from the anointing of the priest and see it as describing the relationship between the One who anointed the Priest and the Priest-king. Like the older commentators it is best to see this as a reference to the covenant of redemption which took place between the Father and the Son in eternity. The Father asked the Son if He would become a man to save the elect and the Son replied that He would. Coming into the world He said: "Lo, I come: in the volume of the book it is written of me, I delight to do thy will, O my God: yea, thy law is within my heart" (Psalm 40:7-8). In His high priestly prayer He began, "Father, the hour is come; glorify thy Son, that thy Son also may glorify thee: As thou hast given him power over all flesh, that he should give eternal life to as many as thou hast given him" (John17:1-2). In eternity He had been given an elect people by the Father. He had come to save them, to lay down His life as the Good Shepherd for His sheep (John 10:11, 14). He was facing the horror of Golgotha, learning obedience through the things which He suffered (Hebrews 5:8), feeling the full pain involved in saving His people. He was obedient unto death, carrying out all that was agreed in the eternal covenant. The counsel of peace or covenant of redemption was between them both. This eternal covenant underlies the covenant of grace which God makes with His elect and their children.

4. The Reward for the Work (v14)

"And the crowns shall be to Helem, and to Tobijah, and to Jedaiah, and to Hen the son of Zephaniah, for a memorial in the temple of the Lord."

The action of these four men is praised. They made a collection in Babylon and brought it to Jerusalem to help in the building of the temple. A crown was made from some of this silver and gold. Initially and symbolically this crown was placed on the head of Joshua the High Priest. Zechariah, having performed the symbolic act of crowning the high priest, the crown is now to be taken and placed in the new temple which is being built. It is to be kept there as a memorial. It will be a memorial of what these four men did. No labour in the Lord is in vain (1 Corinthians 15:58). Jesus taught, "For whosoever shall give you a cup of water to drink in my name, because ye belong to Christ, verily I say unto you, he shall not lose his reward" (Mark 9:41). But it will especially be a reminder to those immediately involved and also to Israel in the days following, of the coming Messiah who will be the great Priest and the great King. The promised Priest King will surely come.

5. Blessed days Ahead (v15)

"And they that are far off shall come and build in the temple of the Lord, and ye shall know that the Lord of hosts hath sent me unto you. And this shall come to pass, if ye will diligently obey the voice of the Lord your God."

As gold and silver were taken from Babylon to make the crown, so from distant lands people will come who will build the last, greatest and spiritual temple of the Lord. The Samaritans were not allowed to join in the building of the second temple, but the Gentiles will be involved in building the eternal temple. This verse is looking forward to the day when, "The Gentiles shall come to thy light, and kings to the brightness of thy rising... thy sons shall come from far, and thy daughters shall be nursed at thy side. Then thou shalt see, and flow together, and thine heart shall fear, and be

97

enlarged; because the abundance of the sea shall be converted unto thee, the forces of the Gentiles shall come unto thee" (Isaiah 60:3-5). The ships of Tarshish shall "bring thy sons from far, their silver and their gold with them, unto the name of the Lord thy God" (v9). "And the sons of strangers shall build up thy walls, and their kings shall minister unto thee" (v10). "Thou shalt also suck the milk of the Gentiles, and shalt suck the breast of kings: and thou shalt know that I the Lord am thy Saviour and thy Redeemer, the mighty One of Jacob" (v16).

The church truly has a bright future. The world looks at the church and despises it. Sometimes we ourselves, in unbelief, focus on the weakness of the people of God, but the great spiritual and eternal temple will be built. It will be composed of a multitude of people, living stones. John writes: "After this I beheld, and, lo, a great multitude, which no man could number, of all nations, and kindreds, and people, and tongues, stood before the throne, and before the Lamb, clothed with white robes, and palms in their hands; And cried with a loud voice, saying, Salvation to our God which sitteth upon the throne, and unto the Lamb" (Revelation 7:9-10). We are to be optimistic. It is not some mere remnant of humanity which Christ came to save. We are told that, "God sent not his Son into the world to condemn the world; but that the world through him might be saved" (John 3:17). So many will be saved that in a very real sense the world will be saved.

The church of God has a great future both in this life and the next. Look with expectation for the great things God will yet do for His church. Think of the words of William Carey, the father of modern missions, who accomplished such amazing work in India: "Expect great things from God, and attempt great things for God." Let us not weary in well-doing. Keep labouring for the Lord and we shall see great things.

THE AUTHOR

REV. WILLIAM MACLEOD, BSc, ThM, a retired Free
Church of Scotland (Continuing) minister, was brought up in
Stornoway. After studies at the Free Church College,
Edinburgh, and Westminster Theological Seminary in the USA,
he became minister of the Partick Free Church (Glasgow)
congregation in 1976. He was translated to Portree (Isle of Skye)
in 1993 and then to Thornwood (now Knightswood) (Glasgow)
in 2006, retiring in 2021. He was Moderator of the General
Assembly of the Free Church of Scotland (Continuing) in 2005,
2019 & 2020, Principal of the Free Church (Continuing)
Seminary from 2002-14 and lecturer in Systematic Theology
from 2017-21. He was also Editor of the Church's magazine,
the *Free Church Witness*, between 2000 and 2017. He is married
to Marion and they have three adult children.

Milton Keynes UK
Ingram Content Group UK Ltd.
UKHW020715170124
436182UK00013B/306